Terrariums:
The World of Nature
Under Glass

Terrariums: The World of Nature Under Glass

By GLENN LEWIS
with photographs by author

Edited By TOM F. PATTY

Published by OUTDOOR WORLD COUNTRY BEAUTIFUL CORPORATION WAUKESHA, WISCONSIN

COUNTRY BEAUTIFUL: *Publisher and Editorial Director:* Michael P. Dineen; *Executive Editor:* Robert L. Polley; *Associate Publisher:* John Huenink; *Executive Director:* Tom Patty; *Senior Editors:* Kenneth L. Schmitz, James H. Robb; *Art Director:* Buford Nixon; *Associate Editors:* D'Arlyn Marks, John M. Nuhn, Kay Kundinger; *Editorial Assistants:* Nancy Backes, Diana Durham; *Production Manager:* Donna Griesemer; *Administration:* Bruce L. Schneider.

Country Beautiful Corporation is a wholly owned subsidiary of Flick-Reedy Corporation: President: Frank Flick; Vice President and General Manager: Michael P. Dineen; Treasurer and Secretary: August Caamano.

4

Contents

chapter 1

A World
Under Glass

A terrarium is a small, glass enclosure where plants grow. While this definition admittedly tells us something about what a terrarium is, it certainly doesn't tell the whole story. For in reality, terrariums are different things to different people; and it would probably be safe to say that there are as many different definitions of terrariums as there are people who have them.

For some, a terrarium is a small scientific laboratory where the processes of nature can be studied under controlled conditions. You can see such terrariums lined up in high school and college Botany departments.

There are horticulturists for whom the terrarium is nothing more than a way to grow special and exotic plants. Apparently, their joy comes from the beauty and interest of the plant itself, rather than from the creation of an eye-pleasing whole.

But for most of us, a terrarium is simply a good way to see the beauties of the real world mirrored in the small world of nature under glass. Here, on a small scale, we can practice landscaping and glory in our garden creations. We can watch for clues into nature's inner workings as we test our green thumb and vie with friends to see who can produce the most breathtaking results.

How Plants Grow

Regardless of the scientific advances that have been made in the last two centuries, for me there will always be some element of mystery connected with life. In fact, it seems that in many instances, scientific knowledge merely suggests how much we do not fully comprehend. This scientific data does, however, give us a good place to begin our appreciation of the mystery.

Within each plant there are two processes at work. The official names for these processes are "photosynthesis" and "respiration." Photosynthesis is a long word which merely means that green plants make their own food from sunlight, air and water. Plants take in energy from the sun, carbon dioxide from the air, and water from the soil to create plant sugars. Plant sugars contain stored energy from the sun and it is this energy which pushes bulbs up in the spring and allows comparatively small roots to split large rocks. Technically, the so-called "plant foods" that one sees at the nursery are not really foods, for they contain no energy. Rather, they merely contain minerals which assist the plant in the chemical processes by which it makes food.

"Respiration" simply means that in much the same way humans burn up calories to provide energy, plant sugars are burned up to provide energy for plant functions.

How Terrariums Work

If your terrarium is a sealed one, what you have, in effect, is a self-perpetuating machine that is run by light. Sealed off and protected as it is, the terrarium is indeed a world entirely unto itself. In the world at large, energy is provided by the sun, carbon dioxide is taken from the atmosphere, and water is supplied either by rain or by humans. Water and minerals are taken in by the roots and passed into the body of the plant. During the process of respiration, as plant sugars are burned to provide energy for growth, the leaves give off water vapor (a process called transpiration). In a sealed terrarium, once this cyclical exchange is established, the cycle is self-perpetuating. Carbon dioxide is taken from the air inside the terrarium and water vapor is given off from the leaf surfaces. When the water vapor condenses on the glass walls, drops form and it begins to "rain" down into the soil. The moisture is taken in by the roots, evaporated through the leaves and the cycle goes on and on. Since nothing passes in or out of the sealed terrarium, this tiny world could maintain its delicate life-support system until the very glass around it decayed. And as long as condensation is present on the glass, you have visible proof that the natural process is performing properly.

In an open terrarium, the same processes occur, except that the exchanges are made with the outside world; and you, rather than the rain cycle, must be responsible for providing sufficient moisture.

In a practical sense, terrariums work because they maintain a higher level of humidity than is normally found either in the open air or in our houses.

8

While it was once thought that nature threatened to overcome man's tenuous hold on his territory, now it is nature which seems endangered. Surrounded by glass and seemingly as fragile as the glass itself, the delicate plants seem threatened by buildings all around it.

ight plays with the terrarium,
asting moods in darkening shad-
ws. Sunbeams, which touch the
lass softly, lay down leafy shadows,
reminder of a forest glade. Within
he glass, hourly changes bring
ew illusions of hills and dales, of
ool and mossy recesses, and sun-
t slopes appear. Who can resist
ut for a moment wishing that
hey were small enough to go
alking within the world of nature
nder glass.

We are sometimes led to believe
hat "wonder" and "discovery" are
he exclusive property of a child.
et, surely these can and should
e gifts that last a lifetime. Anyone
who begins the terrarium adventure
s sure to find a world which is as
ipe for wonder and discovery as
he larger world was upon his
irst observation.

Although terrariums are not new, having been in existence
for more than 100 years, they are more popular today than
ever before, decorating shelves in department stores, plant boutiques
and windowsills of homes around the country. There are
several reasons for this sudden upsurge in terrarium interest.
For most of us, the days are gone when we could travel to the
countryside easily. Even backyard gardens and green vacant lots
are less plentiful. Consequently, many people understandably
long for that touch of nature which seems to grow more remote and
inaccessible daily. Terrariums return that touch in miniature. Woodland vignettes, gardens and scapes of all sorts — landscapes,
mountainscapes, and seascapes — can be reproduced in
miniature and brought into the living room. Just as scenes of water are
popular wall hangings in dry countries, the terrarium seems to be more
popular as our view of and accessibility to nature becomes decreased.

As the population density of our cities increases, more
and more people live in multi-family dwellings — apartments and
condominiums — which provide no private garden or yard areas.
Consequently, for people who want to grow flowers and plants,
indoor plants and terrariums are the answer.
To some extent, ecological interest has helped foster plant interest.
The sudden recognition that the natural environment is not an
unlimited resource which can be disposed of and replenished as
easily as we dispose of many of the commodities in our
society, has sparked an unprecedented interest in plants, especially
house plants. Although the idea of saving the wilds by bringing
plants into our houses may not seem completely rational, it is certainly
an indication that one's sympathies are with the preservation projects.
Grandma, we are told, was able to grow lovely houseplants
easily. So now, every weekend thousands of her grandchildren
flood nurseries and plant boutiques, bringing home armfuls of
plants with high hopes that somehow they will discover the
secret to Grandma's green thumb. Yet, unfortunately, many of
these people discover that all but a few of the really tough ones
curl up their leaves and in successive stages of regression, finally
give up the ghost. For such people, terrariums are a perfect solution.
You see, Grandma's expertise was less a matter of magic than
you might think. Since she lived before the days of central
heating and the air conditioner, her rooms were cool in the winter;
and in the summer, the humidity entered the house through the
open windows. (As you might suspect, central heating and air
conditioning tend to produce air which is more suitable for
humans than plants.) Also, Grandma used a lot of water, which
created a very high level of humidity. Open wash tubs and water
and stew pots boiling on the stove were all part of her daily
life. I remember that Grandma's winter windows were always
steaming with condensation.

Condensation falls like fresh rain
as the sun warms a propagating
terrarium in the late afternoon.
This rain cycle is established as
water vapor given off by the leaves,
condenses on the glass. The moisture falls back into the soil, is
transmitted through the plant to
the leaves where it is once again
released into the air as water vapor.
As the cycle continues, the plants
inside divide to divide again and
again to the delight of all who see it.

The untamed Northwoods forest
floor depicts the harmony and de-
sign of the natural world. The
woods should be studied frequently
as an example of how to arrange
your terrarium. The decaying twigs
will help make food for the plants
around it, and the moss, the trail-
ing dogwood and Linnaea will
profit by the windfall.

This terrarium has the look of age.
Plants have waxed and waned over
the years; some have died, their
remains shaping the earth and
providing food for the victors. Some
of the plants in this terrarium were
born in this container and have
known no life outside the walls
of the glass.

Another factor which contributes to the rise in popularity of the
terrarium is the time element. Many people in our modern-day
world are simply too busy to tend a garden, even if they had
one. Terrariums, while not absolutely carefree, require so little
attention that even the busiest of people can manage one with ease.
It seems that the American people are going through changes in
what they value. Moss, for example, stirred the heart of hardly
anyone a few years ago. Now, it is being given more than a
second look. A part of nature that was once taken for granted
is now being enshrined upon the windowsill.
All this activity is a healthy reminder that the natural environment is not an unlimited resource, and if we want our grandchildren to
be able to enjoy it, we must take care of it with love and intelligence.
There are, no doubt, people who will claim that the terrarium
is simply the latest craze or fad. However, logical reasoning seems
to contradict this argument. For one thing, a terrarium is more
of a method than a fashion. Although various types of glass enclosures may come and go according to the styling of the day's
fashion requirements, the basic terrarium will be around as long
as people wish to grow the more delicate, more interesting plants
in rooms with dry air. Because this method works easily; is
adaptable to continuous styling and technical innovations such as
the development and use of plastic materials; and since the method
requires little expense and limited maintenance,
it can hardly be labeled a passing fancy.

The Meaning of Ecology

Ecology is a word that has been so tossed and bounced about by speakers, writers, and advertising men, that a great deal of public confusion has resulted; all this confusion about a word which (if our future is important) should be as clear and sharp as the view of a hawk's eye from on high. In fact, anyone who gets a good grip on the full meaning of this word does himself and future generations a great service. Ecology is not a simple concept like "preservation" or "good management of the forest." It is, rather, an area of science devoted to the interrelationship of organisms and their environment. Thus, like the words medicine or law, it covers a broad, wide-ranging field.

We are often told that ecology means "the balance of nature;" and while this is almost right, it is enough off the mark to lead to confusion. Actually, the balance of nature is only one of ecology's subjects and not the whole thing. A balanced ecology is quite as it suggests—a relationship between the organisms and an environment in which each organism aids or does not interfere with the survival of any other.

Let's consider how a balanced ecology might be upset. In Florida, there is a swamp which contains many grand and unique plant species. Sometime ago, there was a proposal to run a saltwater canal through this swamp. While the canal was but a fine line through a great expanse, ecological study suggested that hurricanes would whip salt water upon the grasses. Although the grasses were not sensitive to the salt, the microscopic algae which grew upon it was ultra-sensitive to the chemical. And this algae was so linked to the food chain that half the area's population might be destroyed if the proposal were approved.

Within each ecosystem, every species has a particular place or niche. A niche is a particular position in an ecosystem where it can function without competition. An open niche is an invitation for some plant to fill it and adapt; and few niches are open for long. Adding a new species to an ecosystem where there is no niche for it to fill means that it will probably die even though other conditions are right. This is why many garden flowers cannot grow in the wilds; there is no niche for them and superior competition forces them out. It is possible, however, for a newly introduced species to have a competitive advantage and force out species which have held their niche for as long as a million years.

Since a terrarium is a closed ecosystem, you have a perfect opportunity to observe firsthand how the various plants relate to each other and to the environment as a whole. You can aim for a balanced system and evaluate your skill; you can find out whether you can introduce new species to fill niches; and perhaps most importantly, you can gain a better understanding of the interrelationship of all living things—an understanding which can then be applied to the world at large.

chapter 2

How to Create an Original Terrarium

Although the official definition of a terrarium is a "small enclosure or closed container in which small plants are grown," one soon discovers that in practice this definition is neither very important nor necessarily very useful. After all, why draw restrictions around creativity? Why be fenced in by a definition?

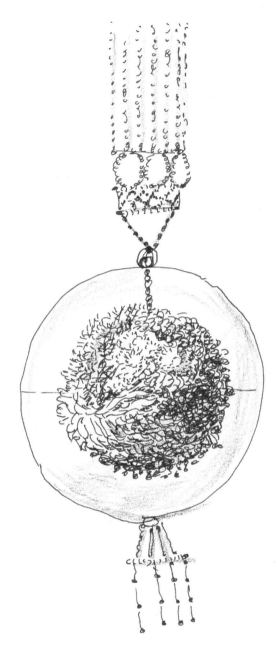

Hanging Ball made from
Ball of moss and chicken wire
two plastic covers glued together
with rubber cement — easy
to take apart if required.

18

There is no reason why a terrarium must be small. Conceivably a terrarium could be as big as a bread box or even as big as a house. In a way, the whole world is a terrarium and we are inside it.

To be creative, you must let your imagination go without limit before settling on the practical. "But there must be some boundaries of definition," you say. "Otherwise, one could start with a garden-in-a-jug concept and end up with a walk-in greenhouse!" This is true. In fact, I know a man who did that very thing. And, incidentally, he is very happy with the way it turned out. Yet, it is a fact that a terrarium and a greenhouse are not the same thing. So, in the final analysis, one must work with restrictions.

If this seems like a runaround, it is; but with a key point about creative thinking. In making things, fine results are frequently achieved by letting the imagination run roughshod over restrictions. Imagine a wall-to-wall terrarium set in your living room floor, for example. Then, return to the practical, restrictive facts of the matter. Switch back and forth between these two worlds as often as need be. The dreams will feed your down-to-earth ideas.

The same terrarium seems quite different when viewed from different vantage points. In the photo below, we see a few sticks and some greenery on a plastic slab; in the photo above, the terrarium has the effect of presenting nature in microcosm.

Actually, this terrarium is a temporary one used for display for a few weeks, after which the plants are returned to propagating terrariums. The short-term terrarium makes many special arrangements possible while providing an ever-changing scene. Such terrariums are especially nice for the holiday season and parties, in lieu of flower arrangements.

Dish Gardens
on blocks of wood
housed in a
plastic Box

20

If you were to listen to a group of professionally creative people having a brainstorming session, you would find their thoughts likely to leap from the hidebound to the outrageous. "Let's make a combination terrarium and bathtub. You could take a shower and water the plants at the same time." Silly, to be sure. Yet, one cannot know ahead of time what good ideas will be revealed behind clouds of seemingly nonsensical thinking.

Once a basic idea has been either discovered or created, the rest is mostly work, with common sense providing the guidelines. You should, however, keep your flights-of-fancy running as you perform the practical steps. This way, when you start the project, you will find that ideas for details will flow as easily as water from a well-primed pump.

I once turned a group of professional artists to thoughts of terrariums. Many sound ideas came from our game. While the terrarium/bathtub sporting came to no useful end, a vision of a terrarium as a giant building housing 50 acres of land did.

Moss Landscape
with stainedglass
background in shades
of blue and violet.

One member of the group knew leaded glass techniques and sketched house shapes which he knew could be made. An abstracted shape, looking the least like a house, was best liked. Another fellow suggested that a blue, stained-glass construction be hung inside to represent the sky—his idea harking back to the vision of a huge landscape enclosed. I suggested that the planting be but a flat sheet of moss, not to detract from the sculptural quality—as our terrarium seemed destined to become a living sculpture.

A color sketch brought up the question of the base. Flat to the table? On legs? The happy idea chosen was wood because it could be painted with enamel in a rainbow color progression—red, orange, yellow, the moss holding the green, and the glass "sky," the blue.

Likely, creative talent is no more rare than plain looking people. It seems rare because most get the dreamer scared out of them. The trick is to get it back and use it. It is still there, without a doubt.

Maybe part of the reason we are afraid of our lavish dreams is that we all know dreamers who never come back to the practical steps required to get things done. But the creative trick is to fly away for ideas, catch them, bring them home and put them to work.

Yes, the cut and dried is safe. You will have a pretty terrarium if you simply drop some partridgeberry vines in a glass candy jar and shut the lid. And, in its way, the effect can't be beaten. It is warm, homey, and altogether lovely on a winter's eve. But, it is a thrill to create something quite your own, too.

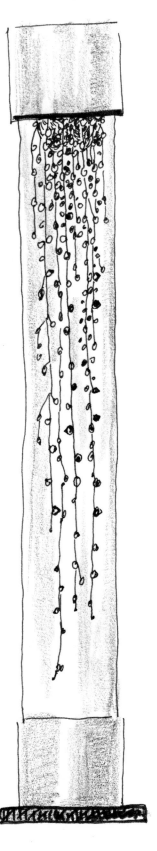

21

Bead plant, a vine in a Tall plastic Cylinder.

chapter 3

Terrarium Basics

Creating A Benevolent Environment

If the extent to which terrariums can be developed seems new to most people, it should be recognized that the basic idea has been around since 1829.

It seems that Dr. Nathaniel B. Ward had tried, without success, to grow the delicate bog ferns in his London garden, speculating that the smoke and pollution produced by the London factories had made it impossible. Now, in a laboratory jar, these delicate plants were growing just as though they were at home in their native bog. Since the same fern that had failed so many times in his garden was now flourishing, he was determined to find out how far the idea contained in this chance success could be developed.

During the next three years, he tried a wide variety of difficult-to-grow plants in glass cases and met with continued success. They grew grandly. Furthermore, he discovered that contrary to the popular misconception that plants need fresh air, these plants would grow for years unattended, with neither additional water nor additional air. Moisture and proper elements contained within the air were apparently produced automatically. The only other problem — one of determining the correct amount of light — was quickly solved by trial and error.

The nineteenth century was the great period for collecting plants from around the world. Plant collectors were public heroes. And for good reason. They did journey to remote places, risking shipwreck, tropical disease, and, too commonly, headhunters, for the chance of sending home valuable species. More often than not, however, their work was all in vain because the plants regularly died in transport on the long ocean voyages. What didn't succumb to heat or cold, lack of light or too much of it, died from the salt-laden air.

Determined to put his findings to the true test, in 1832, Dr. Ward filled two large glass containers with ferns and grasses and sent them off to Sydney, Australia by way of the Cape of Good Hope. After eight months at sea, enduring severe temperature changes, storms and salt-water baths, the plants arrived at their destination intact and thriving; no more upset than if they had spent the time on Ward's laboratory shelf.
Ten years later, Ward published his findings in a book entitled, ON THE GROWTH OF PLANTS IN CLOSELY GLAZED CASES, which recounted his experiences and boasted of his ability to maintain a bottle of ferns and mosses in perfect shape without watering for eighteen years.

In 1829, Dr. Nathaniel B. Ward, a London surgeon by profession, stumbled onto the method of placing plants in small, glass-protected homes quite by accident. Being a natural history buff, Dr. Ward wanted to observe the emergence of the adult sphinx moth from its chrysalis. To accomplish this, he planted the chrysalis in a glass jar containing soil. Sometime later, he noticed that a fern and some grass seedlings had sprouted inside this glass jar. At this point, he apparently became more interested in the fern than in the emerging butterfly, for historians make no further mention of that event.

As a result of this revelation, the popularity of these new plant containers, called Wardian cases, grew rapidly. By the middle of the century, plants in Wardian cases were being shipped all over the world. Plantsmen around the world rejoiced. The tea and rubber growers were especially appreciative, for now they had a way to ship plants and thus extend their plantations to the most ideal localities throughout the globe. In addition to their value to commerce, Wardian cases met with acceptance in the Victorian home; and likely, the heavily-furnished drawing rooms of the period could use the touch of greenery and grace that these early terrariums afforded. Also, the idea that man was able to exercise control over nature, subduing a hostile environment, was a comforting idea to many people in that age. As an example of how times change, today many suspect that it is man that is hostile to nature; not the other way around.

During the past 100 years, Wardian cases have spawned a great variety of light-admitting enclosures for living things — everything from jug gardens to aquariums to plexiglas constructions — many of which Dr. Ward could not have been able to conceive. Although there is an official distinction between a Wardian case and a terrarium (depending upon whether it is used outside [Wardian] or inside [Terrarium]), today most people call them terrariums, even if a qualified "sort of" or "more or less" would be more precise.

Planning your Terrarium

As a first step in planning your terrarium, consider the specific kind of climate you want to produce and control so that you will subsequently be able to select suitable plants for this environment.

Climate refers to the characteristic weather for any given location and is made up of such elements as rainfall, temperature variation and the amount of sunlight a specific area receives for a given period of time. You should ask yourself whether your terrarium's artificial climate will resemble that of a tropical rain forest or that of a low desert region.

Since terrarium environments can and should resemble natural environments, it is a good idea to take a moment to examine the various types of environments which can be created within a terrarium.

1. Tropical Rain Forest Floor. This is the jungle bottom where it is always moist, always shady, and the temperature is constant. No wind blows. Ferns, mosses and certain kinds of bromeliads — all natives of this type of environment — will flourish in the closed terrarium just as they do at home in their natural environment. The plants of this level are usually deep green in color, grow relatively close to the earth and seem always to be dripping with moisture.

2. Tropical Rain Forest: Halfway Up the Trees. Here plants and conditions are quite different from the jungle floor. Plants grow on trees. Air circulation is good, there is more light than on the jungle bottom, and while the humidity is high, plant roots dry between waterings. Plants from this environment require an opening in the terrarium for good air circulation, a requirement which makes it more difficult to achieve the high humidity level that these plants need. In this group are orchids, bromeliads and some kinds of cacti and cacti relatives.

3. Tropical Forest: The Treetops. Yes, there is a group of terrarium-size plants that makes its home here where there is plenty of sunlight, night moisture and frequent rains. As with the plants of the jungle floor, these plants will grow easily in a terrarium. While they need filtered sunlight and a certain amount of air circulation, they do not require the continuously high humidity that the other jungle plants do, enabling you to plant them in partially opened containers. As long as they get sprinkled on the mornings of sunny days, they are fine. Morning watering is advised because the plants should dry by night to prevent root rot. Plants from this environment, such as tillandsia, usually bloom well and have light or grey-colored leaves which tend to be tough and hardy.

4. North Temperate Forest. Here the temperature goes well below freezing in the winter. However, many plants from this area, especially the yellow and grey lichens and pink oxalis, will survive in a closed terrarium without the natural cold. Weak winter light can be duplicated by a lamp which is lit regularly. Plants from the Pacific Coastal forests seem to work best for long-term growing; however, these plants are practically unavailable unless one lives in that area.

5. Semi-Desert: Sun. Of course these plants require a very high light level, but not as high as one might think. These plants can be rested during the winter months of low light and brought to active growth during the bright light of spring and summer, the reverse of their natural situation. A partially open terrarium, with some humidity, is a good way to compensate for the dryness of their natural environment. The dry resting season should not be bone dry; keep the soil slightly moist. During the growing season, the soil should be kept moist but allowed to dry between waterings. This environment should never have a standing-water wetness. Plants that grow well in this environment include cacti and other succulents.

6. Semi-Desert: Shade. Since all desert areas are relatively bright, this group can benefit from full winter sun and bright summer shade. Rains come to this area in season, and it can be quite damp for several months. The terrarium top should allow air to pass, but a good humidity level is beneficial. Many succulents in this group are not particular about rest periods or periods of wet and dry. You can let them dry between waterings. Haworthias are one good example of precisely such a succulent. Ferns, mosses and various leafy plants from shady, semi-desert areas offer a chance for an odd and rare type of terrarium — one that goes totally dormant in the summer. You simply store it in a basement or closet during its rest period. With the terrarium lid secured, the soil will remain quite dry, but the air will retain a trace of moisture. In the fall, a little water will bring it quickly to life again. The Pacific Coast has many lovely plants of this type. I have used the small, semi-desert ferns as potted plants, as well as in terrariums. In fact, some plants from this area may be dried and brought to life again several times a year. At the present time, however, they are unavailable except in their natural environment. However, I will offer these ferns as spores to the seed exchange of the American Rock Garden Society for the season beginning January 1975, and anyone with a strong desire for them can get them through the membership listed in the back of this book. Growing directions for fern spores will be found in the section on ferns.

7. Bog or Swamp. Many fine rushes, sledges and grasses from this environment make for highly artistic terrarium arrangements. Mosses and a wide assortment of seldom-seen plants are common to the swamp. Many, particularly the rare ones, are available only through specialty houses. I advise planting sphagnum moss, which is green, odor free and easy to manage, in a closed terrarium.

8. Water and Bank. This is a situation where water surrounds a bit of land like an island. In a terrarium, the island can be a large rock. You merely arrange your soil on top of the island and plant. In most instances, this type of environment is restricted to the very large terrarium. In fact, the one I made some 20 years ago was in a 60-gallon aquarium. A filter system was required to keep the water clear and the top needed to remain partially open to prevent the plants from decaying. Maintenance is high for this type; but when this kind of terrarium is lit at night, it can be most dramatic.

9. Cool-Weather Type. This type of terrarium environment is for those who have a sun porch or unheated room where the night temperature drops to the mid-40's during the winter months. Since the cold allows considerable sunshine without overheating the terrariums, many kinds of flowering plants can be grown with the extra humidity the terrarium produces. Miniature geraniums, roses, and small bulbs will grow well in partially covered terrariums.

10. Alpine. These are the plants which grow above timberline on high mountains. And although it is possible to create such an environment in a terrarium, it is, in reality, almost totally theory. Controlled cold is required during the winter months and a cool location must be found for the summer.

Once you have determined which type of environment you want to bring into your home, you can begin to think about the specific terrarium you will create. Depending upon the specific environment you want, you can choose between an open and a closed terrarium.

25

Closed Terrariums

If you want to create a forest floor environment or a bog climate, you will need a closed terrarium. This is the only way you will be able to achieve the high humidity level required. There is constant moisture present in the sealed terrarium because after an initial watering a constant rain cycle is established. As we pointed out in Chapter One, moisture is taken into the plant via the root system, passes through the leaves and eventually evaporates into the air. The evaporation condenses on the glass walls and "rains" back into the soil to repeat the cycle. Therefore, theoretically, a sealed terrarium should be self-sufficient.

Open Terrariums

Depending upon the size of the opening, an open terrarium allows some degree of air circulation. And although the humidity level is considerably less than in a closed terrarium, it is still much higher than in the air outside the container. Since the perpetual rain cycle is not present here, open terrariums need to be watered and watched more closely than closed terrariums. Depending upon the particular container that you use, an open terrarium may have a very small opening, like the opening of a five-gallon water bottle; or the opening can be quite large, like an open aquarium. In between these extremes you have everything from brandy snifters, to glass cookie jars, to simple glass fruit jars.

Water

The quality of tap water varies considerably from city to city. So many important factors, such as the chlorine content and the quantity of soluble salts and minerals in your water, will depend upon where you live. However, if it is not common knowledge that you have a water problem in your area, chances are that you don't need to worry.
If you do have a problem with your water, there are several means of dealing with it. A chlorine problem can be solved merely by allowing the tap water to stand overnight in an open container. During the night, much of the chlorine will dissipate. Warm water contains less chlorine than cold water, and since plants will not be harmed as long as the temperature is kept at a reasonable level, here is another solution. If your water is salty or contains high levels of minerals, you will know because alkali and other salts will appear as a white crust upon the soil. If this occurs, you will have to use bottled water or rainwater.

Water and the Closed Terrarium

For the closed terrarium, watering problems are most effectively solved by getting the original moisture content correct. The general rule is to water as little as possible. If condensation is present on the glass, you should have sufficient moisture. As we have indicated, theoretically, you should not have to add additional water to a sealed terrarium.

Water and the Open Terrarium

In an open terrarium, the rate of evaporation varies according to the size of the opening, a rate which is increased if the terrarium is placed in a very warm room or near an open window.

The key is to watch your terrarium closely until you understand its drying pattern. If the opening is large enough for you to put your hand into the terrarium, the finger method is best. Stick your forefinger down into the soil about an inch or so. If the soil is damp, it isn't time to water yet. If the soil is dry, add water. The soil should not be allowed to dry out completely, so check frequently.

If the opening is too small for your hand, you will have to become an astute observer. If the plants appear limp, if there is no condensation present on the glass, or if the soil appears to be light in color, your terrarium needs water. If wilting has occurred, it might be too late.

The vast majority of people err in overwatering, not underwatering. And since too much watering can be even worse for plants than too little, it is necessary to exercise caution. If you overwater, either in terms of quantity or frequency, the plant roots will become waterlogged and will begin to rot away as your plant decays and eventually dies.

Soils

Soil is the foundation upon which your terrarium is built, and the kind of soil you put in your terrarium could determine whether your plants grow and flourish or wilt and die.

For the true terrarium aficionado, soil should be made at home. Following is a list and a brief description of the soil components you will need to make a very light, disease-free, easy-to-mix soil.

Perlite is expanded volcanic rock whose lightweight particles provide for good drainage and airing.

Vermiculite, unlike Perlite, does not facilitate drainage; instead, it retains moisture and soluble nutrients.

Sphagnum Peat Moss is a form of undecomposed bog moss which provides for good aeration, drainage, water retention and nutrients.

Mixing Your Own Soil

You will need to buy and mix one part sphagnum peat moss, one part perlite, and one part vermiculite. To every quart of this, add a tablespoon of limestone chips or crushed eggshells.

If this sounds like too much trouble, you will be pleased to learn that many commercial growers have developed artificial soil mixes which work extremely well for nearly all terrarium plants. These can be purchased at your nursery and many outlets where terrariums are sold.

I find this mix visually offensive, however foolproof it might be. While the white speckles darken with age, the mix still looks artificial. One way of dealing with this problem is to cover the areas where the mix shows with moss, sand, pebbles, or forest soil that has been steamed in the oven to sterilize it — an unpleasant-smelling process that takes about an hour in a covered kettle at 350 degrees.

Fertilizer

As with water, it is better to use too little than too much. Go extremely easy with the fertilizer you buy, using about one-fourth the amount called for on the package directions. (It is best to use liquid fertilizer.) It is possible to *grow plants* in a terrarium for a very long time with no fertilizer at all. The common practice is to give a plant fertilizer when it is doing poorly. This is a grave mistake. Actually, the proper time to fertilize is when the plant is doing well, usually during the spring growth period when the plant can absorb it and utilize it. If you apply fertilizer to an ailing plant as though you were applying medicine to a sick person, the soil may build up excess mineral salts which will damage rather than help the ailing plant.

Light

Each plant has particular light requirements; and unless these requirements are met, the plants will not thrive.
The most obvious source of light is sunlight, especially if you plan a windowsill terrarium. If the light source is sunlight, however, there are several things to keep in mind. Since plants tend to lean in the direction of the light source, it will be necessary to turn the terrarium around periodically so that all sides get equal attention. Sunlight transmitted through glass can produce intense heat, and on a hot day a closed terrarium which is placed in front of a sunlit window may turn into an oven, actually cooking the plants inside. To prevent excessive heat build up, ventilate it frequently, removing the lid from time to time. If you spot algae growing inside your terrarium, this is a good indication that the sunlight is excessive.
There are, of course, varying degrees of sunlight, ranging from full sun (any southern exposure) to heavy shade. As a general rule, it is safe to say that the more direct sunlight a terrarium receives, the more necessary it is to have periodic to constant ventilation. Full sun, partial sun (eastern exposure) and filtered sun (through a curtain or glass screen) locations should be reserved for open terrariums only.

Sunbeams are especially dangerous if the plant is in an otherwise dark or shady location. One hour a day of direct sunlight may be enough to kill an otherwise healthy plant.

Artificial Light

In areas where there is insufficient sunlight, you will have to use artificial light. Because they remain relatively cool, fluorescent lamps are better than mercury vapor or incandescent lights; and the new color-corrected tubes are the best of the fluorescents. Fluorescent light should be placed close to flowering plants (within a few inches). They may be more distant from non-flowering plants, but in no instance should the light be more than about eighteen inches from the plant.

Plants need periods of darkness when they can rest. Most plants require about eight hours of darkness; but flowering plants, especially during their dormant period, need more and foliage plants slightly less.

Temperature Range

The proper temperature range for most terrarium plants is between 50 degrees and 85 degrees Fahrenheit. In most instances, the terrarium temperature will be very nearly room temperature, the only exception being those terrariums which receive direct sunlight.

Problem Solving

There are only a few problems which you are likely to encounter with your terrarium, and the chances are slim that you will face even these. However, when and if you do run into trouble, it is best to know how to handle it.

The most common problem with the terrarium is mildew, caused by an excess of moisture. The solution is quite simple — just remove the top and allow the plants to air out. If the mildewed plants are severely damaged, it is probably best to remove them and replace them with new ones. Mold, the kissing cousin to mildew, is also caused by excessive moisture; and the solution is the same.

While it is extremely unlikely that your terrarium will pick up any insects or bugs after you plant it, it is entirely possible that there will be insects and/or bugs present at the time of planting, especially if you use soil from your garden. Mealy bugs, white flies, plant lice and scale insects can all be taken care of with insecticide spray. For the aphids and snails, however, you will have to remove them by hand, using a damp cotton swab.

Blackened leaves are caused either by pouring water directly onto the leaves or, more probably, by the intrusion of a direct sunbeam into the terrarium. When this happens, the glass acts as a magnifying glass and before you know it, you have a burned leaf.

If the leaves turn yellow, either the humidity level is too high or the light level is too low.

Here is an idea for a home-built terrarium/aquarium made from plastic. The plants grow on islands which have been cemented together with silicone cement to form planting pockets. This type of construction allows the island to be lifted completely out of the container without disturbing the plants when you have to clean the aquarium.

The plants are mosses, swamp plants and tropical rain forest plants — all plants which accept very high humidity levels. It is possible to grow orchids in this container if the light level is sufficiently high.

Since tropical fish must have water which is heated to a degree that would deter plant growth, gold fish are used instead. The number of fish should be severely limited so that you do not need an air pump. Given the large surface area, sufficient oxygen levels will be produced by the plants. Actually you do not need to use fish at all; water snails and frogs are quite suitable for such a set up.

It is possible to achieve a similar result by using a regular aquarium tank which will have the advantage of coming ready-made and equipped with lights. The main problem here is that more light tends to create more algae and will discolor the water. However, if you plant the surface of the water heavily with duckweed or water lettuce, the algae content will be severely reduced.

Be sure that all rocks are well cleaned before you put them into the container. Be careful to avoid using porous rock that might have been exposed to insecticides. All plants should be washed thoroughly before they are planted to make sure that no poisons have been brought from the nursery.

The soil must be free of poisons or heavy fertilizers. If in doubt, straight sand or sphagnum moss may be used as a planting medium. Peat moss is another soil which is recommended here.

chapter 4

Plant
Selection

A wide choice of dwarf begonias is available for terrarium plantings. As the photo demonstrates, begonias provide interesting stem and leaf texture as well as color. The small flowers blossom in hues of red, green, silver and pink. The begonia seems comfortable in either an open or closed terrarium.

Because the world's plant variety is enormous, there is seemingly much material to choose from in making a terrarium. However, since only a small percentage of the plants found in the world, much less the typical nursery, is suitable for terrarium life, you must choose with care, consideration and caution. "Suitable" means some 2,000 or more species, depending upon how you rate them. You should keep in mind, however, that this figure represents the number of species that will work in all kinds of terrariums. It includes all manners of terrarium environments from desert to forest types, and all light levels from low to high.

Consequently, plant choices for any particular environment in the small terrarium is rather limited. Of course, your selection can be increased considerably if you are willing to hunt in rare plant nurseries and among fellow hobbyists. In fact, wild-land scouting while traveling, particularly to tropical places, can add adventure to a trip and will almost always produce some unique finds.

Plant choices for the various environments and light levels range from a high of about 400 species for filtered, all-day sun, to a low of about 15 to 25 species for a well-lit room but away from windows. But again, this number depends upon how the plants are rated and the extent to which one is willing to scour plant sources for greater choice. One point should be clear, however. The plant choice increases as both the size and light level of your terrarium are increased.

Most people restrict their ambitions to small terrariums which use the low light levels found in most places about the home. And although the plant choice for this kind of terrarium is relatively small, mostly the mosses, ferns, and such plants that make their home in the deep forest, there is still quite enough variety for a great range of achievement.

In selecting plants for the smaller terrarium, be wary and be aware. You'll need plants which thrive in this tight environment and will remain to size scale. Ironically enough, most plants suggested by print, nurserymen and florists, grow far too big and far too fast for these small containers. Some otherwise fine publications fault on plant selection in photographic examples and plant material guides. Many of the plants which are shown and suggested are fast growing jungle varieties with mature sizes ranging from 3 to 30 feet. With anything approaching proper growing conditions, they will stuff the small terrarium and pop the lid off in a matter of weeks. So, be sure to check on the mature size of your plants before you buy.

Do not rely completely on the average nurseryman for help. Few are terrarium practitioners. He will, in good faith, suggest juvenile plants from his general houseplant selection — the same group his other customers use for terrariums. Few but the knowing would question this group because it is the same group florists use for their gardens in brandy snifters. They do look fine in shops and the single plants are not expensive. In fact, they are commonly used precisely because they are most profitable to raise and sell, being attractive and fast growing. This group will flourish in the home, most withstanding nearly all manners of neglect. And although you may never complain about plants growing too well, you should recognize that you will have little control over these fast growers.

Pictured is a dwarf begonia suitable for terrariums.
There are between 30 and 40 dwarfs currently available in the trade.
People can write the Begonia Society (listed in the back of the book)
to find out more about the special hybrids.

Sometimes referred to as the
Strawberry geranium, this
Saxifraga sarmentosa has
been experiencing a revival
of popularity in the plant
world. This plant forms
runners like a strawberry
and produces new plants at
stem ends. It will do well in
filtered light.

The Prayer plant (Maranta leuconeura kerchoveana) has leaves which
fold together at night. This plant, with its bushy growth, makes an
excellent background plant. It will do best in filtered light with high humidity.

Erodium Chamaedryoides (Roseum) is an attractive plant which is commonly used to cover steep banks in hot, dry areas. But, interestingly enough, it also grows well in the moisture of a terrarium. If the plant is given sufficient light and good air circulation, the plant will bloom intermittently all year long. Don't hesitate to experiment with plants that seem illogical for the terrarium environment; you will be pleasantly surprised.

This hybrid, Rechsteineria X Sinningia, is representative of an almost ideal group of flowering terrarium plants — the Gesneriads (the family to which the familiar African Violet and Gloxinia belong). Not all of the Gesneriads are suitable for terrarium life, but enough are that the family is surely in the forefront of the terrarium plant choices. (New hybrids especially bred for the terrarium are coming in yearly.) An added advantage of this group is that nearly all of the plants can be easily propagated by leaf cutting. Adventuresome horti-culturists may try seeding some of the new hybrids to see what interesting results can be achieved.

Fittonias are fast growers which will grow under the adverse conditions of low-light levels, infrequent attention, and minor abuse. Their speedy growth makes it more difficult to achieve a neat, tightly controlled terrarium; but if you like the jungle-like effect of tangled and weedy rompers, this is the plant for you. After all, all terrariums do not have to be neat to be attractive. Fittonias can frequently be purchased in super markets and dime stores. The crisply marked leaves come in bright pinks and carmines as well as whites and greens.

This particularly exquisite Ixora species was located in the "Closed-to-the-Public" section of a rare-plant nursery — a possible indication of its availability. Furthermore, the nursery had only this one specimen in stock and refused to part with it. The Ixora genus is well known for its bloom.

The Maranta genus sports some of the most colorful and sharply patterned leaves in the plant world. Fortunately, most of these plants are very easy to grow under terrarium conditions, although many are so tall that they are appropriate for large enclosures only. Most house-plant nurseries have several types available. The flowers are small and white.

Several varieties of grand miniature geraniums are possible considerations for the large terrarium, including the tiny-leaved, scented ones as well as the flowering types. If you can provide the proper temperature range (about 50 degrees at night; less than 70 degrees during the day), you should have no problems with these plants in terrariums. Keep them in cool rooms; keep the soil on the dry side; give them plenty of light, and keep them pinched to shape.

A Peperomia species spins its round leaves like pads on a wire mobile. Delicate in substance, it grows well at low-light levels.

These African Violets are unique in a manner which is not readily apparent in the photograph. The leaves are tiny—some no larger than a dime. Violets, both full size and the dwarf varieties, do exceptionally well in the terrarium. Keep the container partially open to avoid condensation because the soil should be kept a bit dryer than regular pot culture.

This is a dwarf form of the Dracaena species. Full-size dracaenas are frequently used as houseplants because of their tolerance for typical home conditions. But the nearly perfect example shown in the photograph owes its quality to terrarium conditions. The golden color in the sheen, however, is not a quality of the plant but is, rather, a reflection of a nearby automobile.

chapter 5

Container Choices

CONTAINER CHOICES

Any transparent container which will hold water and can be easily opened and closed can serve as a container for your plants. And a quick glance around any major city should reveal a number of astonishingly different choices, as new terrarium designs seem to hit the market almost daily.

Most terrarium builders feel a pull in one of two directions; either the terrarium is conceived as a piece of art, in which case the container is not just a container but an essential component in an artistic creation; or, the terrarium is viewed as a horticultural enterprise, in which case the container becomes almost of secondary concern. If your tendency is in the direction of "terrarium as art," you should feel free to use anything that will be aesthetically appealing. If you care about the horticultural side at all, however, you will want to be aware of several limitations which might restrict your thinking on containers.

For one thing, colored containers, even those with extremely muted colors, will severely reduce the light intensity. In addition, colored glass tends to transmit its own color onto the plants. In other words, a green glass will transmit green, and a red glass will transmit red. If you use a red glass, the chances are that your plants will become elongated and leggy, since the light at the red end of the color spectrum seems to have this effect on plants. And if you use a green glass, the green glass will block out the red and blue light, without which no plant can live. Therefore, unless you are willing to restrict yourself entirely to low-light level plants, shy away from colored glass containers of any sort, including wine bottles.

Glass or Plastic Containers

In all cases where you have the option of choosing between plastic and glass, I recommend using glass. Although plastic has a definite weight advantage, its susceptibility to harm from scratching seems to outweigh this slight advantage. Almost all of the plastic containers which I have seen (with the exception of those made of Lucite) have become scratched within a short period of time and generally, they appear somewhat cloudy, not crystal clear.

Glass Containers: Aquariums

Of all the glass containers available, aquariums are certainly the most available and quite possibly the least expensive for their size. Large tropical fish stores have rooms full of rectangular containers — everything from small, two-gallon sizes to incredible (and expensive) one-hundred gallon capacity tanks — which are perfectly suited for terrarium conversion. All those terrarium-makers who were once tropical fish fanciers will be glad to learn that the ugly steel-edged reinforcements which used to accompany aquarium tanks have gone, the glass now being glued together to give smart, crystalline edges.

Because of the large production and distribution facilities available for these containers, they can be purchased for relatively little cash, with prices ranging from around $5 for the small, two-gallon size to more than $30 for the 30 gallon size. If you're looking for a bargain, try to find an old, used and possibly leaky aquarium that represents evidence of a few months of tropical fish fever. A small investment for a tube of aquarium sealant will turn this into a luxury terrarium. When looking at aquarium tanks as possible terrarium material, it is best to look for a tank which is tall and skinny, rather than the low, wide models. Not only will these aquarium containers more easily fit on top of your windowsills, but they will also be more attractive when they are filled with plants.

Bowls, Glasses and Jars

Of course, oversized brandy snifters, old goldfish bowls and cookie jars are traditional terrarium containers. But to this list, you can immediately add beer mugs, flower vases, juice pitchers, jelly jars, bottles of any size and shape and old glass coffee pots, too. However, keep in mind that the wider the opening, the more moisture your terrarium container will lose.

42

Here is a representative sample of some of the plastic boxes which are suitable for terrarium conversion. One of the boxes pictured here has a mirrored back; another, while originally intended for a small sculpture, could easily hold a potted plant as well.

One of the more original and interesting variations of the bowl terrarium is a dome terrarium. This is merely a bowl which is inverted to cover plants that are set on a tray or in a pot. Glass domes like the ones which were once fitted over wax fruit and stuffed birds in Victorian parlors are especially good finds. But you had better make sure that you get to these antiques before the antique dealer does; otherwise, they will cost a small fortune.

Bottles

Before you hide your empty five-gallon Sparkletts water bottle in the closet as the container for a future terrarium, you should realize that such small-mouthed bottles and jars make for the most difficult-to-plant terrariums possible. To be sure, some of the interest in these bottle gardens is a carry over from the ship-in-the-bottle days when you spent hours trying to figure out how they got that big ship into that two-inch opening. If you can resist the urge to reminisce, select another container. However, the people who are interested in bottle gardens can take a close look at "How To Make A Bottle Garden."

Plastic Containers

There are several manufacturers who make plastic boxes which are suitable for terrariums. The boxes may be used as open or closed terrariums, depending upon whether you add a lid. Some plastic supply houses offer raw materials so that you can fashion your own terrarium. The main skill required here is in clamping the pieces together during the drying of the weld.

Miscellaneous Containers

Makers of stained glass have indicated that they would make custom terrariums if given at least two months notice. Be prepared to pay heavily though. Expensive glassware makes elegant terrarium containers, especially for very nice gifts, since when and if a person's terrarium days should end, the glass can revert to its intended function. Containers should be selected with two thoughts in mind. One, "What kind of plants will go inside it?" and two, "How will it look in a room?" Whether the opening is small, large or otherwise, will determine what kind of plants you put in it. And how the given container will look in any given room is a factor which will require some experimentation and thought.

A Moss Covered Log

Props For The Terrarium

If the live plants in a terrarium are the feature players, additional items might be called the stage props, and should, just as on a real stage, serve to enhance the realism of the creation.

Props for the Terrarium

44

Piece of driftwood

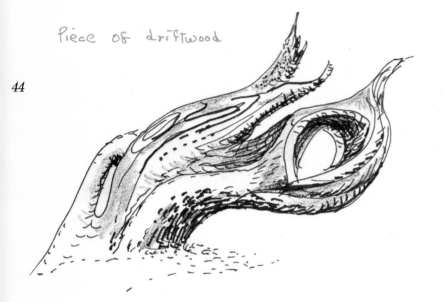

Wood

Wood, of course, is one of the best natural props for any terrarium, especially pieces of old wood from the natural woods. These are often moss covered and, if they have begun to decay, they will provide an excellent surface on which to grow many other plants. However, since many pieces of decomposed wood contain insects and fungi, you should soak the newly collected wood in a bucket of weak insecticide. If you feel this is too much trouble for an old piece of wood, do not plant valuable specimens in decomposed wood. A similar problem occurs with driftwood, as this type of wood frequently contains salt minerals. All driftwood should be soaked in fresh water for at least a week to leach out all salt. Wood props should look natural, as though they had fallen off large trees years ago. Old twisted roots which rise above the soil as though a large tree were standing nearby, is one way to achieve this kind of natural effect.

Shells and Shell Chips

Shells and shell chips, like sand, can also be very effective in conjunction with succulents for seashore scenes. However, be careful not to overpower the scene with these props. In reality, seashore vistas are about the only possible occasion where you can use either white shells or white sand in a terrarium. In all other landscapes, the white becomes an irritating distraction from the naturally softer colors of the plants.

A Moss covered Barkchip

A Moss-covered rock

Rocks

Rocks can be used to provide additional texture and color. Some of the porous types are especially good as surfaces upon which to plant moss and small ferns. Using rocks in this manner allows you to achieve various levels of interest by providing a terraced look. Rocks can also be used as background foils for foreground plants.

And finally, the hard and seemingly timeless rocks provide a sharp contrast to the soft, ephemeral plants. In general, it is best to use rocks of the same type. Try strenuously to avoid the "rock collection" effect.

Moss covered Pebbles

Sand

Two of the more attractive uses for sand are the miniature brook bed for a woodland terrarium setting, and, in combination with succulents, as a desert or seashore environment. Frequently, a layer of natural sand against the aquarium glass is more attractive than soil. (Remember, however, that sand should not be used in plastic containers because plastic is too easily scratched.) Although many naturally colored sands exist around the world, they are not easily available and you will probably have to resort to the colored sand you find in tropical fish stores. As a general rule, these sands are too artificial looking to bring out the best in your terrarium.

45

Pebbles and Gravel

Pebbles and gravel can be used to provide textural effects, or for the more adventurous, to make avenues for small brooks and streams. You should be extremely careful here to avoid any kind of mathematical placement or else your terrarium will look plainly artificial.

Various Sands + pebbles

Misc. Rocks

Man-made Props

Ceramic statuary of artificial composition, bridge representations, and other such man-made objects, require a very special handling so that they do not look pretentious or silly. Only in a carefully scaled, beautifully composed scene will they work. And if there is the slightest doubt in your mind about the appropriateness of such items, it is best to leave them out.

chapter 6
Special Plant Groups

This fern-populated, three-year-old terrarium looks so healthy in its open container that you should know all the facts before you try to achieve similar results in your apartment or home. Actually, this terrarium has been kept in a greenhouse where the still air, even temperature, and high humidity create just the right climate conditions. The glass bowl you see serves merely as a portable showcase.

Ferns

It is an interesting fact that among the most suitable terrarium plants are the most ancient of plants: the ferns, mosses, club mosses, and selaginellas — all spore bearing and dating back before the age of flowering plants. In fact, almost all the plants of this early period are likely candidates for terrarium culture. Perhaps they have lived so long and been so successful at it that they are flexible in requirements; or perhaps they evolved in such dampness as the terrarium affords. In any case, the ferns are a major plant group for terrariums.

The list of fern species is very long, containing plants from every conceivable environment from the frozen Tundra to the tropics;from the damp areas beneath waterfalls to the nooks of semi-deserts; from full sun to the most shadowy of places. It's no wonder that some species are ideal for the terrarium.

Many species are either too large or require too much light to be practical for the terrarium, but this still leaves many smaller species.

48

New ferns will spring from spores which alight upon a section of palm fiber in a greenhouse. Within the terrarium, ferns will also propagate when spores drop on unoccupied areas of soil.

four-times larger-than-natural close-up reveals the incredible detail that makes ferns one of the world's most beautiful plant families.

A plant which quite possibly conveys the most etherial, delicate feeling of all the world's plants, the Adiantum hybrid (Misty), is easier to grow than it looks. It does, however, need to be placed in a closed terrarium of sufficient size which can maintain temperatures under 70 degrees during the winter. In any case, this beauty is worth the effort.

A simple potting mix or woodland-type soil will work for most sorts, as most kinds are happy with a slightly acidic, medium soil.

Light requirements vary and need testing out according to the specie; yet, any given fern will usually work in a broad band of light condition so long as humidity is high.

How To Grow Ferns From Spores

The growing of most kinds of ferns from spores is a lesson in simplicity itself. This method allows you to obtain many plants which might not otherwise be available in full-growth form. Also, it allows you to have many baby ferns for special effects.

Some firms offer spores for sale, but the best method is to gather spores yourself by collecting the brown dust on the underside of fern leaves. The most effective method of gathering these spores is to pick the whole frond, or part of it, and place it in an envelope to dry for about a week; after which time, the spores can easily be rubbed off. Then, place the dust-like spores in small packets inside sealed glass jars.

Spores, unlike seed, are not fertilized. They contain only half the genetic information needed to produce a whole fern. When planted, they make a green growth called a pro-thallus, and this produces male and female organs. It is not until the egg, which is produced by the prothallus, is fertilized that a fern can develop, no matter how long it might grow in that form. All fern leaves do not bear spores, nor are they always dust-like ready when you want them.

Before you sow the spores, you should first sterilize the soil; either bake it in a covered dish or buy it in a sterilized form. If you bake the soil, you can place it directly in boiled plastic snap-lid refrigerator jars to avoid any air contamination while it cools. When the soil cools down, sow the spores and seal the glass jars. Place the jars in well-lit, but out-of-the-way areas, and forget about them for several months. Without further attention, the ferns will grow until you are ready to plant them in larger containers.

Late winter and early spring sowings make for much faster results than those planted in the fall or winter. A temperature of about 65 degrees Fahrenheit is ideal, but most will grow in temperatures somewhat higher.

Doodia media, a dwarf fern noteworthy for its symmetrical growth, is suitable for medium-sized terrariums, ten-gallon size up.

52

This silver dollar Maidenhair-fern deserves a terrarium
housing all of its own, especially since it is almost impossible to
grow these beautiful ferns without the very moist conditions of a
terrarium. These large ferns — some 2 to 3 feet in circumference when
mature — will be the focal point in any room.

This Polystichum setiferum multifidium is a hardy fern with leaves about 5'' long.

rely the royal family of all ferns, the
antum, is apt to grow too large for the
rarium. The best solution is to plant in
all pots hidden beneath the soil. Not only
I the confines of the pot restrict growth,
t the pot may be lifted out, the fern
vided, and a reduced section of the plant
n then be returned to the terrarium.

This Pellaea Rotundifolia, or Button fern,
has round, dark-green leaflets which
ntrast sharply with normal fern foliage. This particular plant
does best with filtered light and high humidity.

These dish gardens pictured here were specially designed for terrarium life in plastic boxes. The moss was gathered from an area only feet from my home, and no scar was left. Within weeks after the moss was removed, the area was green again with new moss. The larger, leafed plant pictured with the moss is Liverwort, a moss relative. The planting trays are from bonsai supply houses.

The Mosses

The single, most appropriate plant group for the terrarium may well be the lowly mosses. Moss, a very simple plant which is able to live at extremely low-light levels, can provide the miniaturized effects of lawns, meadows and tree-covered hills as nothing else can. This look is achieved by planting various kinds of moss in an evenly spaced way.

While many northern mosses may not live long without their natural cold season, warm-climate mosses from moist green areas will flourish indefinitely in the terrarium. These hardy plants can be found by looking underneath the benches of commercial greenhouses. Here you will see moss spores from tropical locations that have found a new home where the temperatures are constant. Special sorts of moss may become more available from terrarium supply houses as the demand for moss increases. In fact, several Japanese nurseries around the Los Angeles area are offering special strains of moss spores for Bonsai hobbyists. Another good way to obtain special mosses is to join a Bonsai society such as the ones listed in the back of this book. Also, any collected moss from woodlands is worth the terrarium test.

Unless you want an instant effect, you do not need a great quantity of moss to start with. A small amount may be dried and crumpled upon acidic, high-humus soil. Planting can be done in plastic, snap-lid jars. Just snap the lid and set the jar aside on some well-lit (not sunny) spot. Left alone in this condition, the moss form will be ready for terrarium planting in about six months.

This moss, transported directly from the famed moss gardens of Kyoto, Japan, is of the sun-loving variety and now covers the roots of a bonsai tree.

Falling between the developing branches of the moss, the club mosses and the ferns, this Peacock Selaginella sports a unique leaf coloring among plants. Although this plant will grow at low-light levels, its blue tones become more pronounced as the light level is increased. In good light, the leaves change to bronze and copper tones. Like its allies, the mosses, selaginella propagate by spores, although horticulturally it is propagated by cutting. Any of the various varieties of selaginella make good terrarium plants.

This mountainous-looking extravaganza is composed of thousands of single moss plants which fit comfortably in a four-inch dish. It is best to keep such dishes inside the terrarium; otherwise, you will have a problem with watering. In order for the moss to remain in this lush state, the soil must be kept moist.

This particular Selaginella species is a real beauty — a slow-growing plant which sends shoots upright in woody stalks before branching into ferny foliage.

One small Northern wood can produce an astonishing variety of mosses. The plants pictured here, including the mosses and gray lichen, came from a small woods in upper New York State. Lichens, while often grouped with mosses, are really quite different. Lichens are a combination of fungi and algae which behave as a unit rather than as a single kind of plant.

The illusion of wealth is given by an apparent mound of the semi-precious stone Lapis Lazuli, purchased at a rock-and-mineral store. While rare stones are usually out of place in the regular terrarium, moss seems somehow to make the scene believable.

Like most Stapelia, this one (Stapelia gigantea) blooms well even wh[...]
it is only inches high. The Stapelia gigantea can produce a bloo[...]
eleven inches across. The plant is dormant in the winter, and requir[...]
strong, filtered light for bloomin[...]

The Fernwood Nursery of Topanga, California.

58

Succulents

Succulents are not only one of the most available plant groups, but with their fanciful forms and exotic appearance, they are also one of the most attractive. Many kinds of succulents can be found in local nurseries and even in some markets and 5-and-10¢ stores. The more unusual kinds can be obtained through various succulent mail-order houses listed in the back of the book.

While succulents have earned a reputation for growing in the hottest, driest and sunniest of places, they will flourish in the moist terrarium if the light level is sufficient. The explanation for this apparent irony is that plants do not always choose the ideal location in nature; rather, they live where they can. Consequently, the commercial propagating nurseries place succulents in shady locations with unnaturally high humidity. In the home, however, I would recommend that succulents be given all the full sun possible except in the summer months when partial sun can be substituted. This will insure good form, proper leaf structure and excellent color and bloom. Succulents with green leaves can usually get by with less light than those with built-in sunscreens which take the form of a coating of white or bluish powder or a thicket of thorns. Succulents should never be moved from indoors to full sun outdoors without at least a week of conditioning in bright outdoor shade; otherwise, the plant will be sunburned for sure.

Terrariums housing succulents should never be fully closed. Air circulation is important to help avoid root rot and to prevent the soaring temperatures created when any closed terrarium is placed in the sun.

The soil should be a very lean mixture of one part humus to ten parts coarse sand. The missing nutrients can be supplied by a very small amount of liquid fertilizer. If this mix is three or more inches deep, the succulents can be kept in small, buried pots of clay (not plastic). This tends to restrict the overgrowth which retards blooming and allows you to remove the plant if it should become infected. By using clay pots, you can water the soil around the pots during the best season and the moisture will be absorbed in a correct amount. A slightly moist soil is appropriate for most months; however, during the late fall and the dark of winter, succulents should be kept just damp enough not to shrivel. This kind of underwatering will not likely cause harm. Overwatering, however, will cause soft, elongated growth which is very susceptible to rot — a condition which must be strenuously avoided with succulents.

59

This small plant, geared to withstand a hard desert life, sprouts a bloom of glory. The technical name is Ariocarpus Kotschoubeyanus, although it is more frequently referred to as Roseocactus Kotschoubeyanus in the trade.

These Stone plants (Lithops) can be grown easily if given adequate sunlight. Your best bet in finding these plants is through one of the catalog houses. The plants are most effective when planted in quantity so that one may compare all of the delicate differences. Accustomed to infrequent rains, seeds germinate in a matter of hours; the sprout quickly shaping itself into the compressed form of an adult to store the maximum amount of water. By seeding you will be able to obtain hundreds at a low cost. Be careful — these whimsical plants are extremely sensitive to rot caused by overwatering.

Haworthia nitioula is one of the most attractive members of the shade-loving Haworthia species. Haworthias, grown mostly for foliage form, are extremely tough and enduring plants. A favorite of mine is Haworthia truncata which is thick and compressed in the manner of Lithops; and like Lithops, truncata has transparent window areas on its flattened top.

Many small cacti will flower on a sunny windowsill; but since the blooms do not last very long, it is best to arrange your setting so that the main body of the cactus provides the interest and the bloom is a bonus. Pictured is the Rebutia senilis — an excellent genus for terrariums because of its small size and the quantity of its bloom.

Although this plant has a similar appearance to the large, desert Yucca, this small plant is a Sedum mutticeps. Unlike most Sedums, it does not sprawl, grow too quickly, nor does it require winter's cold to keep it compact. As one might guess from the small amount of leaf surface which is exposed to light, it is used to strong light. One can often guess the requirements of a plant by its structure.

This is a Glottiphyllum oligocarpum, a stemless, succulent perennial.

The Huernia genus includes many attractive, small
succulent species with comparatively large blooms. This
one is Huernia vansonii. A succulant is not a genetically
related group of plants; rather, succulent applies to any
plant which stores an uncommon amount of water. It is
a descriptive term like small or round. Since water storage
is related to dry conditions, succulent plants are usually
grouped together because of similar cultural requirements
and a similar appearance.

63

Senecio rowleyanus, or Bead Plant, nicely bridges the gap between the popular houseplants and those plants which are suitable for the terrarium. While its leaf-strung vines will roll around the small terrarium's floor, it should be allowed to hang down several feet.

How to Plant a Bottle Garden

64

1. Assemble all materials. Materials should include: wooden planting sticks which have been notched at the ends (planting sticks can be fashioned from pencils, chopsticks, coat hangers, etc.); a rolled paper funnel; a small watering can with a spout; and a spraying mechanism (a used Windex bottle is good). Other tools which are shown on the sidelines will be explained as we go along.

2. First, make sure your container is clean and dry. Then, using the funnel, pour the soil ingredients into the terrarium container. The soil should be slightly moist, not completely wet. In this case, charcoal chips from an aquarium supply house go in first, then pebbles, colored sand, and then planter mix. Pebbles and sand are for decoration, but also function to facilitate drainage. Charcoal helps to keep the soil sweet and adds a rich, black color.

3. With one of the wooden sticks, dig a small hole. Lower the first plant into the jar with the sticks and adjust it into place. It is advisable to use small plants which fit comfortably down the small opening.

4. Using a small toy shovel or part of a spoon tied to a stick, you should do some spade work. Cover the plant roots with soil dug from the next hole you intend to fill.

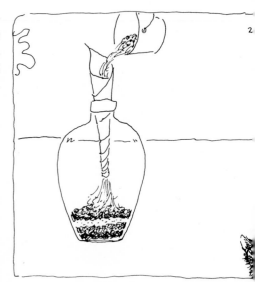

5. Make a "tamper" by tying knotted rags to a stick. Use this tamper to firm down the soil around the plants. Then repeat steps 4 and 5 with each plant until all the plants have been placed in the soil.

6. A useful item for gripping rocks and other objects which do not object to the sharp pinch is called "Flexible Finger" or "Astro Finger." Since the ends are rather sharp, it is not recommended that you use this instrument for placing plants.

7. Pour in the colored sand to add a stream bed, making sure that the paper funnel is rolled tightly to insure accurate pouring.

8. In a very short time, your bottle garden will look like this — lush, full and green. And you will assuredly be asked how you did it.

3 Months Later

Those who take frequent trips into the woods w
be able to appreciate the details of this setting. T
wilderness provides a gallery of possibilitie
The inquisitive may discover ideas for futu
terrariums; the harried may seek peace a
inspiration; and the philosophical may question th
discrepancy between man's materialistic opulence ar
the simple beauty of moss and a fallen berr

chapter 7

Wild Plants

Collecting Wild Plants

Collecting your own terrarium plants from the wilds can be very rewarding. However, this is an extremely tricky area of activity involving the law, objections from concerned citizens, and a real threat to some species which have a very tenuous hold on existence. Much is not settled about the actual threats involved in general plant collecting; and it is an area of mixed fact and fiction, mixed emotions and genuine concern.

In researching this question, I have checked opinion and procedures with representatives of the U.S. Forestry Department, local sheriffs of wild-land areas, botanists, park rangers and citizens active in conservation work. There is wide and often near violent disagreement among people who would ordinarily be united in a common goal.

One school of thought argues that nothing should be removed from the woods: no plants, no bloom, no seed, no fallen stick — nothing. Some people of this stripe, soften this absolute to say that people should be allowed to take seeds. This "remove nothing" view is quite widespread.

Another school of thought argues that the removal of a few plants from the wilderness will not endanger the plant population. These people are quick to point out the fact that most plants have an enormous capacity to deal with all of the mishaps nature can throw at it; and that, furthermore, plant survival is fundamentally predicated upon the continuation of an environment as a whole, not the loss or gain of a few individual members. On this issue, each person should make up his own mind. But let me put forth my own observations and beliefs.

In the first place, there are a few — very few — cases where a small plant is just barely holding its own in the wilds. And these plants are usually in unique areas where conditions are unusual — in sand barrens, on top of lone mountains, or in areas where a combination of mist and coolness is unique. Usually, such plants are growing very slowly, moving to an evolutionary dead end.

So, some rare species are rare because their environmental conditions are rare. And a few other species are diminishing rapidly because foreign species have been introduced to take their place. However, most of the rare species which are on the losing side of the numbers game are there as a result of the activities of man. As man changes his environment, he changes the natural environment around him. Yet, plants seem somehow to struggle back, even against the onslaught of man's activities, as long as the environment as a whole has not been tampered with. For example, roadsides which are scraped clean of vegetation will, in a few years time, be carpeted with nearly every plant logical to that area and sometimes in greater numbers than before. When small areas are overturned to make ponds or swamps where there was none before, all the plants common to swamp areas are quick to appear, including such rarities as orchids. The point here is simply that plants grow when the environment is right for growth, and as long as this environment is not altered, the plants will continue to propagate.

A plastic cake cover makes a dome for displaying
woodland mosses, wintergreen, and a small hemlock
at holiday time. Such plants may be gathered even
in the deepest winter if one can find them beneath
the snows. While the arrangement is not intended
to be long lasting, as indicated by the lack of a
water- and soil-retaining receptacle under it,
occasional sprayings with water will keep it going
for many months. After use, the mosses are valuable
as a covering mulch for regular houseplants.

69

Looking at the larger picture, I would have to agree with those who say that in the majority of cases, plant collecting by responsible and intelligent people will not endanger plant populations. Yet, almost immediately, one realizes that there is a long list of exceptions which should accompany this statement. Rather than listing all these possible exceptions, let me include a few general rules which should be followed.

First, any species which is not seen in mass should be left alone.

Second, public parks, wildlife parks, small, unique, or close-to-the-city areas which are already under strain should be left completely alone. As a general rule, collect from large land tracts rather than from small, easily-upset areas.

Third, never collect more than the few plants you fully intend to use. And never collect for friends. You can be responsible for your own commitment, but not for that of other people.

Fourth, stop collecting if you find that you lack the skill or the proper motivation.

And last, but not least, never collect for resale or profit. Such commercial ventures have actually swept wide areas clean for a generation.

When collecting, always work with a field book. There is hardly an area in the country which is not covered by one. The book will help you decide whether or not to take a particular plant.

The best method I've found for the "how to" of collecting is to come prepared with a digger and some plastic bags. Dig up all the roots, shake off the soil, and place your plants into the plastic bags without water. Evaporation from the plants themselves is quite enough, and additional water might cause rot to form in broken parts before they have a chance to heal. Once you have collected the plants you want, tie your bags. You'll find that they are quite lightweight. The soil can be reconstructed when you get home, or local soil can be carried separately in a small bucket. Protect your packages from sun and heat, and try to get them home as quickly as possible. If you don't take the follow-through steps to keep these plants alive, plant collecting is not for you.

As far as the legal aspects are concerned, it is lawful to dig on private lands if you have the owner's permission. Always make sure you have received this permission before you start digging. Government land is often a good collecting spot, but ask the local sheriff first. National Forests and Parks are not totally out of the question. You will need proof that the plants will be used for educational purposes, and you will need to give a good indication that you know exactly what you are doing.

Before you begin, remember that done properly, plant collecting is real work, and unless you are horticulturally motivated, you should do all your plant collecting with a camera, not a shovel.

Located near a spring in an otherwise semi-desert canyon, this wild
Pacific Maidenhair fern stays green all year round while its less fortunate
sister plants suffer drought upon the bone-dry hills. Many plants will perform
better and longer in artificial settings such as terrariums than in
their natural environment.

Small tree seedlings placed inside a container fashioned from an old light fixture
make a simple yet festive globe. Such trees will survive through the winter, to be
planted outside when spring comes.

A Trip Through the Woods

Somewhere between the fall of autumn leaves and the fall of snow, Mary would schedule the Terrarium Session — a big event for the children of our neighborhood.

Mary was ancient (at least 50), but by her devotion to nature, authority of having once taught 1st grade, and vast travel experience (she'd been to Europe twice!), she was exactly the right kind of girl for a 7-year-old to court and win. Her house was sprawling — 25 rooms — with plants in every one of them. Windowsills were jammed with vines, ferns, cacti, rooting things, things in jars, and fantastic terrariums. Rich by depression standards, Mary made her own soap, collected everything (What else is a large house for?), and dressed habitually in such near rags that strangers thought she was the maid. We children knew her true richness. It lay in her closeness to all things that are a delight to the child — bird's nests, rocks, seasonal changes, details of the grasses, and above all, terrariums. For this, we forgave her lumpy cookies and her occasional lapse into commerce with the adults who came from miles around for the color she added to their lives through plants.

So, upon some snappy morning before the snow claimed all green but the dark of pines and hemlocks, Mary and our troop would set off through the barnyard and towards the woods with bags, diggers, and the superfluous scarves which our mothers had insisted on. Mary would point out the plants and tell us their names and special qualities. In return, we'd point out the rime-crusted mudholes as if we were wiser about walking than she.

There were bluets and violets near the swamp to bloom on February windowsills. Partridgeberry, whose red berries would grow redder and fatter with each month in the terrarium, could be seen under the pines. Mosses gone unnoticed in summer's fullness were now seen as a superlative in lushness. There was prince's-pine and running-club mosses, small fur trees and arbutus and an occasional rattlesnake plantain which Mary said was an orchid's best friend in the woods. And there was wintergreen.

With the morning gone, we'd dash to our respective homes for the food mothers also insisted on, then back to Mary's for the actual terrarium making. Those adults that Mary bothered with would be there asking questions and calling each other "girls," but the children would have their own special work table.

Jars of all kinds would sparkle on the kitchen table. Woods soil was in a bucket, the plants in baskets, and newspapers were spread all over. Mary's "girls" brought cut glass jardinieres and fish bowls. We had commercial pickle jars from Mary's vast pickle jar collection.

Compost went in first, then the plants. We made a lot of jolly noise. Partridgeberry was the favorite of Mary's "girls," and Billy didn't much care what he got; I liked wintergreen — its red berries having the advantage of being eatable should one be sent to bed without supper and have no other recourse against starving than to raid the terrarium.

Mary would admire our work from time to time with honest phrases like, "Why that's the most beautiful terrarium I've ever seen!" I would be critical, "Ruthie didn't get her roots down. She just stuck moss on top." Then, Mary would give me a knowing pat and wink.

We'd always make a few extra terrariums for people in the hospital. We took Mary's word that there were such things as hospitals and people in them, although I couldn't understand why adults who had no interest in terrariums when well should suddenly covet them when ill. Mary said, "Because they have time." Then, we'd haul out Mary's vast collection of candy-box bows and pick just the right ribbon for the gift terrariums.

When all the afternoon's work was spread out upon a cleaned kitchen table, it was a lovely sight. "What do you think?" said Mary to me. I said, "Why do you old ladies call yourselves girls?" Mary said, "Because when we are happy, we feel like little girls again." I nodded, suddenly it all made sense.

The annual Monkey flower is dwarfed in the wilds by very limited soil on a damp rock face. This suggests the use of annuals to perk up a terrarium planting for a brief but colorful change of scene, dwarfing them to terrarium size by using less than ½ inch of soil. You might try sowing seeds of small, fast blooming sorts upon porous rock. Clarkia is an approporiate choice to try here.

Pale December light glances across a woodland vignette featuring wintergreen, club mosses, and moss covered bark in a New York apartment window. These plants remind the owners that their snowbound cabin will be ready with the coming of spring.

The summertime berries of Clintonia (blue) and a ground-creeping Dogwood (red) can be used in summertime terrariums by city folk who find the wildwoods too distant for regular visits. Taken up in the earliest spring, these plants should perform in the terrarium until early winter. When I use such Northern plants, I return them to the woods for winter or store them in the refrigerator for several months.

The Venus Fly-trap hails from the Carolinas and enjoys filtered light during its summer growing season. Dormant roots can be purchased in the spring from plant shops which deal in novelties. If you keep these plants in small pots and store them in the refrigerator during the winter, they will last a long time.

Carnivorous Plants

Whether one considers them beautiful or ugly, everyone seems to agree that carnivorous plants are striking and bizarre. Adaptation to insect trapping as a way of life has led to unusual forms and colors not found in the leaves of the more common plants. Frequently, the leaf is colored in shades of maroon, red, and apple green. Plants of the same species may grow side by side, each with a different coloring. When well grown, some carnivorous plants have a textural look that is most unusual, almost as if they were made out of plastic.

Darlingtonia, with its hooded tube, is reminiscent of a striking cobra and is sometimes called, and not surprisingly, the Cobra plant. A native of California, the first specimens were snatched by W. D. Brackenridge of the Wilkes Exploring Expedition — snatched rather than collected, because at the time, Brackenridge was retreating from an Indian attack on the slopes of Mt. Shasta.

Insects are attracted to the Darlingtonia's orifice by the honey-bearing glands within. These glands are interspersed with downward-directed hairs which prevent the insect from crawling out the way it came in. If it tries to fly out, it flies toward the light; but since the Darlingtonia's hood is bespeckled with translucent window spots, the insect is once again stopped. Ultimately, tempted by honey further down, the insect moves to an area so smooth that no foothold is possible, and it eventually falls into a digestive liquid which is excreted by the pitcher-like walls. At this point, the insect is absorbed into the lower portions of the leaf.

One may wonder why a group of plants would go to such trouble to evolve complicated trapping mechanisms when green plants can make their own food. The answer is that the chemistry of swampy areas often ties up the nitrogen in an insoluable form, making it unavailable to the plants. Therefore, insects are essential to plants because of their nitrogen content.

The Drosera, or Sundew, is a small plant which comes in tones of red and green. It is especially beautiful with each leaf hair topped with a sparkling drop of honey. Australian varieties are somewhat larger and a bit easier to keep than the American natives. The sticky honey traps tiny flies as the leaf closes down upon its prey.

The Sundew (Drosera) plant requires high light and humidity levels to stay healthy. Pictured is the Australian species, considerably larger than the American species which, when full grown, has leaves about one inch in length. The small flowers come in red, white or pink.

The Pitcher Plant (Sarracenia) does not have the hood of the Darlingtonia, but it has downward-directed hairs and honey glands which work in a similar fashion.

I have had success by growing Darlingtonias, Droseras, and Sarracenias in live spahgnum by keeping the covered terrarium under trees in the summer and at a temperature of around 45 degrees at night during the winter months.

With a movement that is much faster than the Drosera, the Venus-Flytrap, or Dionaea, closes with a snap that startles the eye. The spiky rim resembles a set of jaws. Hinged in the center and activated by small trigger hairs upon the leaf's surface, the spikes slowly close until they form an interlacing barrier around the insect. Then, with the cage formed, they shut with resolution, not to be opened again until the insect is but a few crumbs of skeleton. This plant requires some air circulation to avoid rot and also requires more sunlight than the others of the insectivorous group.

My own favorite carnivorous plant is the Pinguicula Caudata. It is especially notable for its bloom and the fact that it produces two kinds of growth — a small succulent rosette which is about one-inch in diameter during its winter resting period, followed by leaves about four-inches long and two-to-three inches wide which last through the summer. While it is true that some Pinguicula entrap insects with movement at the leaf surface, the Pinguicula Caudata seems merely to hold out its leaves like tongues. And since the leaves are covered with a sticky fluid, small insects adhere. If the Pinguicula Caudata is placed in the terrarium, the terrarium should be open and placed in an area that gets plenty of summer sunshine. By fall, the growth will begin to deteriorate until it forms the resting rosette again. It may be propagated by breaking off the small, rigid leaves of the rosette cycle; the broken leaves placed flat in pans of sand for rooting. Although the plants need to remain wet, drainage is important and must be good. Do not water the leaves because it will remove the natural fluid deposited on the leaf's surface.

The Pitcher Plant (Sarracenia) comes in different hues of greens and reds. In order to get these plants to bloom, you should keep your terrarium outside during the summer months. The plant requires very moist conditions.

The Butterwort (Pinguicula) has attractive flowers of yellow and blue. The leaves are covered with a sticky substance to which insects adhere. This plant will do best if planted in moist rock gardens.

chapter 8

Children and the Terrarium

Children And The Terrarium

Most children want instant success, and yet, at the same time, they usually appreciate the excitement of constant discovery that accompanies slow development. Terrariums conveniently satisfy both seemingly contradictory desires. Once the materials have been assembled, terrariums can quickly be made and the results can be instantly seen.

Terrariums are something a child can own, a little world under his dominion. Furthermore, a child may feel that he can involve an adult in his project.

By children, I'm thinking of those between the ages of 3 and 8. After 8, most young people can manage terrarium making and the study of it quite well by themselves. Some children are quite ready for a terrarium at age 3; although, if the child is going to own it and carry it around, it must be plastic. Then, should the terrarium be dropped, the plants can be moved to another container. Soft plants that break should be avoided.

Perhaps the best thing about terrariums for children is that success of some order is almost a sure bet. Closed, the terrarium can go unwatered, and if it is kept out of direct sun and given bright shade, little can go wrong.

If you plan a terrarium-making affair, include more than one child so that it can be a real event. You'll find that children of all ages will be interested.

If possible, take the children with you when you buy or gather the plants. It adds a great deal to the adventure and stimulates thought about what kinds of plants to select — an exercise in observing differences.

Set up a table where dirt will not be too great a problem. Insist on giving a demonstration first. Spell out all the important ground rules before you begin because once you get started, it is very unlikely that anything you say will be heard.

Do not be surprised at the speed with which children work. However, you should not extend the project beyond a child's attention span. Praise is important, but a critical eye is appreciated by most children. Praise indicates that you were pleased, which pleases the child; a critical eye shows you cared and paid enough attention to consider the qualities of the work.

Seeds work well in a child's terrarium. Usually, the results are short lived, but much can be gained by watching the germination and the development of green leaves. Beans are another favorite. For a long-term spectacular, use an open terrarium with one sensitive plant — a mimosa which germinates readily and grows quickly with filtered sun. The leaves, being sensitive to a touch, fold up while the stems fold down when touched. Frequently, touching one plant will often cause the whole group of plants to collapse, as the closing leaves of one activate the next. Don't be discouraged. Within a short time, the leaves will rise again.

Children will need help in placing their terrariums. It will be your job to find the proper light level. I remember that as a young child, I once placed a terrarium on a heat radiator thinking it would help my tropical plants. Needless to say, they were cooked the following morning. Also, you can expect children to do things which seem odd to more experienced adults, such as washing the plants with soap or dumping on a cupful of fertilizer. Such mistakes are common and show evidence of a concerned heart and an eager mind.

Animals In The Terrarium

Technically, the addition of animals to your glass enclosure creates a vivarium. However, for the sake of clarification, let us think of the vivarium as those rather dull and

barren cases which zoos and biology classes keep. Such specimen vivariums, even when the animals seem most healthy, have always depressed me. Although the educational reasons for their existence may be altogether valid, these vivariums seem to suggest a caged and colorless life in a poverty stricken environment lacking the variety and richness of circumstance that surely animals, even in the limited capacity we grant them, must crave. A subliminal lesson might be the suggestion that such a lean environment is a fact of life which must, therefore, be accepted not only by animals but by humans who are caged and trapped in barren cities and colorless daily routines. To my way of thinking, this kind of exposure is altogether worthless unless it is accompanied by facts which enrich man's existence and attune him to his place in the scheme of things.

Therefore, I prefer to think of a terrarium with animals as an environment to which the animals are added. In this concept, an element of harmony is maintained and the development of the project manifests the idea of completeness within a limited area.

The first prerequisite for such an environment is sufficient space. Determine the space requirements for any animal used. Two small frogs might conceivably require a 20-gallon tank, while a baby alligator would probably require such a large tank that it would be both financially and spatially impractical for the home. It is unpleasant, both from a humanitarian and an aesthetic point of view, to see an animal touching glass almost nose to tail. On the other hand, it is pleasing to see a small animal moving about in his own roomy, private world.

The second consideration to insure environmental richness is to evaluate the particular habits of an animal and to provide what is required to complete his patterns of normal activity without frustration. If it moves from land to water, sometimes walking and sometimes swimming, give enough of both. If it digs in soil or underwater sand, provide it. If it hops, give it space to hop. If it likes to hide, give it something to hide under.

81

Details of animal comfort should be considered also. Some animals (turtles, for example) like cold during the winter. If you cannot supply this condition in your home, it is best to restrict your animals to the tropical variety.

The tropical forest, the bog, the woodland, the water's edge, and rocky forest cliffs are all good, choice environments for animals who love dampness.

A desert environment for horned toads and desert lizards is probably the easiest to establish and maintain. Here you can use cacti and other succulents, sand, rocks, and perhaps, a bit of dry driftwood. A water supply is required even for desert animals, as is a temperature greater than 65 degrees. The woodland setting used for chameleons, frogs, salamanders, snakes and toads should provide a damp but not water-saturated climate. Water settings require the most maintenance to keep the water clean.

Mice and other rodents are not suitable for terrariums. However, ants, spiders, fish, and turtles seem to adjust to terrarium life easily.

Small tropical frogs are a good bet, as are lizards, salamanders, and toads. They are not disruptive and seem most fitting among the greenery. Some of this group have colorful imports such as green spotted horned toads or red and black banded frogs. Snakes appeal to some, and small ones would fit the very large terrarium as an environmental concept. All of these ground animals eat the same type of live food, usually meal worms purchased fresh from pet supplies or raised by oneself.

I do not recommend animals in the terrarium for any but extremely responsible and dedicated children. Experience indicates that animals are best kept under the supervision of an adult who makes sure they do not fall prey to all manners of innocent and sometimes not so innocent mishaps. Animals which die under irresponsible care provide an education in callousness which is better left unexperienced.

Selecting Terrarium Plants For Various Light Levels

Low-Light Levels

Level One: (Defined as about five feet from a window with an unobstructed northern exposure.)
This is the end of the spectrum where green plants will grow. Below this level, certain plants can survive, but they consist of fungi and other saprophytes which live off the food of undecayed matter. (It is possible to construct a terrarium with such plants, but the horticulture would be most specialized and the results would be quite strange.) For this low-low-light level, one must confine his plant selection to the thin and fuzzy mosses from the deep recesses of the forest.

FUNGI   SAPROPHYTES   MOSSES

Level Two: (Defined as about three feet from a window with an unobstructed northern exposure.) Here again, the mosses are the mainstay of those plants which will remain healthy in this limited light. However, many other plants of higher light requirements will maintain a good appearance for many months with little or no growth until the energy stored up from better times is used up. Ferns, selaginellas, and club mosses begin to have species which will maintain themselves at this low-light level. Plants which work well at this level are nonflowering and tend to have thin, water-filled leaves. The only sure-fire method of knowing which plants will live here is to test various likely species.

FERNS   SELAGINELLAS   CLUB MOSSES

Level Three: (Defined as about two feet from a window with an unobstructed northern exposure.) Here, low-light ferns, mosses and selaginellas start to look reasonably healthy. Plants from the following list (See Level 5) may be tested in this light level as borderline items.

Medium-Light Levels

Level Four: (Defined as at the window of an unobstructed northern exposure or with built-in fluorescent lighting placed 2 to 2½ feet away.)
(For plants requiring medium light with the intensity of Level 4 and/or 5, see the list for Level 5.)

Level Five: (Defined as light from a northern exposure with additional fluorescent lights 12 to 18 inches away.)

*ANTHURIUM SCHERZERIANUM (Pigtail Plant)
*BEGONIA   BERTOLONIA   BROMELIADS
CALATHEA (Maranta)   CHAMAERANTHEMUM
CTENANTHE (Calathea)
CYMBALARIA MURALIUS (Kenilworth Ivy)
*EPISCIA (Peacock Plant)   FERNS   FITTONIA
FICUS REPENS PUMILA   *GESNERIA CUNEIFILIA
GEOGENANTHUS UNDATUS (Seersucker Plant)
HEDERA HELIX (Ivies)   *HYPOCYRTA
HELXINE SOLEIROLII (Baby's Tears)
MARANTA (Prayer Plant)   OXALIS   PEPEROMIA
PILEA CADIEREI (Aluminum Plant)
*SAINTPAULIA (African Violet)
SAXIFRAGA SARMENTOSA (Strawberry Plant)
*SCILLA VIOLACEA   *SEEMANNIA LATIFOLIA
SELAGINELLA (Moss Fern)
*SINNINGIA PUSILLA (Miniature Gloxinia)
*STREPTOCARPUS (Cape Primrose)

Level Six: (Defined as an eastern or western exposure with low sun filtered through a curtain for a few hours each day.)
While this may be a bit too bright for some of the plants in Levels 4 and 5, the flowering plants (designated in above list by an asterisk) in this group will bloom excellently here. Many ferns will also

grow well here. Any terrarium in this light level should not be tightly closed.

High-Light Levels

Level Seven: (Defined as sunlight filtered through a curtain on a southern exposure.)
In this light exposure, bromeliads will start to produce blooms. A few orchids will also flower. Many of the medium-light level plants will also flourish here if they are under the shade of other plants such as ferns. Any terrarium in this exposure should be left partially open.

BROMELIADS   ORCHIDS   FERNS

Level Eight: (Defined as a southern exposure with direct sunlight. During the late spring or summer season, the sunlight must be filtered.)
Here, many orchids will do extremely well, as will bromeliads and succulents. Some annuals will provide a quick showing and the dwarf pomegranate will bloom here. Any terrarium in this exposure should be at least one-half open.

ORCHIDS   BROMELIADS   SUCCULENTS

Level Nine: (Defined as an all-glass room with full sun.)
If the humidity is low, succulents will grow in this exposure. If the humidity is higher, you can grow a long list of sun-loving plants from wild strawberries to herbs. Any terrarium in this exposure should be left completely open.

SUCCULENTS   HERBS   WILD STRAWBERRIES

A Flowering or a Leafy Terrarium: Which Shall It Be?

Usually, one desires to achieve a mixture of both flowering and foliage plants; however, if one views these alternatives as being mutually exclusive, several points could be made.

The leafy terrarium has a select group of plants which maintain good appearance in a wide range of light levels, especially the low levels. Perhaps, because these plants lack bloom, they seem to have something extra — a growing ease or a textural variety — not present in the flowering plants. Of course, the color is limited, but it *does* exist, with color variety extending into yellow-greens, reds, silvers, white and cream, pinks and blues — as in the case of the Peacock selaginella.

The flowering terrarium plant generally requires much more light and care than the leafy terrarium plants. While there is a group of nearly perfect terrarium plants which flower at medium-low light levels and have lovely leaves — notably the begonias and gesneriad group — most of the flowering plants have their seasonal ups and downs. Extreme light requirements, such as those for the bromeliads and orchids, bring about problems of heat build up and air circulation. And as a whole, the flowering plants are more costly; perhaps as a result of these complications involved in growing them. Frequently, one must nurse a flowering plant throughout the year for only a few days of bloom.

As a group, flowering plants differ widely in their cultural requirements. For example, a begonia and an episcia should be kept just barely moist, while a gesneriad needs to be kept wet. This difference obviously creates problems if you want to grow the two together. Consequently, there is a much greater need for careful culture matching with flowering plants than there is for foliage plants, most of which will be happy in approximately the same light, soil and water conditions.

chapter 9

Special Kinds of Terrariums

The imaginative use of a lamp chimney will set off virtually any tall growing specimens to make an attractive terrarium.

The Propagating Terrarium

It is a good idea to reserve one or two terrariums just for propagation. The cracked aquarium that you would otherwise sell at a garage sale will do nicely since the crack will not matter to its new function. A lid fashioned from saran wrap or some other kind of plastic wrapping paper will make a top that can be quickly adjusted to provide proper air circulation for any season.

Two variations are common. One method is to plant leaf and stem cuttings in damp sand on the terrarium floor. Begonias, the gesneriads, and the succulents will root this way. Sand is used because it retains moisture, allows for good air circulation at the roots and remains disease free. Also, sand provides a good contact surface for the cuttings. Don't use very fine sand, however, because it tends to pack down, decreasing the air circulation advantage. Live sphagnum can substitute for sand and should be reserved for more difficult cuttings. Sphagnum has the advantage of extreme airiness and plants can be left longer in sphagnum than in sand before they must be moved to pots.

Another method of propagation is to plant a division or part of an existing plant. You must use a complete section—complete with roots, leaves and growing bud. Usually you will be able to pull the section from the main body of the plant; however, with delicate plants, you may need to cut the plant with a sharp knife.

To protect the plant, apply a fungicide to the cut portions; then, place the division in sand until a new growing tip is formed. When your new plants are healthy and full, you can move them into a permanent container.

This gift terrarium, shown here without its plastic dome cover, is ready to receive fully-grown plants. Such plants can be raised from regular stock rather than using expensive nursery plants.

Extremely small plants are used to pack this candy dish, an excellent gift for the plant lover who knows what choice items it contains. At a later time, plants could be moved to a larger terrarium and the dish utilized for its intended function. This gift contains small ferns, a ficus vine, Sinningia, and Peperomia astrid.

Gift Terrariums

Terrariums make elegant, long-lasting and much-appreciated gifts for people of all ages and all stations in life. Since they are easy to make, are beautiful upon presentation, and since they last much longer than flowers or candy, terrariums are suitable for all gift occasions.

Gift terrariums come in a variety of sizes and shapes. At one end of the spectrum you have the gift of fine glassware into which some plants have been placed for temporary display. At the other end is the simple brandy snifter or converted fishbowl with a ribbon wrapping.

As a general rule, keep your gift terrariums on the small, simple side unless you are absolutely sure that the recipient has both the room and the desire for a larger, more elaborate one. It is best to use strong plants such as peperomia, mosses and ferns.

Plant Boxes With the advent of clear, strong glues which are capable of holding sheets of plastic and glass together without rim reinforcements, the resulting transparent boxes suggest uses beyond the typical terrarium concept. Moisture-loving plants can be grown in pots inside these plant boxes for months and then be removed to decorate the house for special occasions.

In point of fact, the ways in which plants and containers can be utilized and housed within overall containers are just now beginning to be explored. And, no doubt, some very large

arrangements will result.

One especially good use for the plant box is to hold gift plants — those fine greenhouse beauties which so often collapse in the dry air of our houses long before their time. All too often, one sees luscious azaleas, cinerarias, cyclamens, and calceolarias, which have been purchased for the holidays or special occasions, start to wilt within a matter of days. A plant box with a few air holes could keep these plants going for weeks, even without good light.

Scenic
Terrariums

Hand-built props provide an opportunity for the model builder to test his skills at scaling to size. Successful illusions in miniature depend on proper scale.

The bridge which connects an island to the mainland is part of the compositional technique used to provide depth to this scene. The plants are ferns and mosses.

A dry gravel bed suggests water, but the only water here is contained in the porous rocks which supply moisture for the mosses. Notice how the valley helps to create the illusion of increased elevation levels in the mountain.

Raymond Y. Chang, who made the gardens in this special section on scenic terrariums, carries on a tradition of miniature landscaping which began long ago in the Tang Dynasty (168 to 906 AD). Begun as imitations of Chinese paintings rather than representations of nature herself, miniature landscaping borrowed techniques from painting to achieve elements of composition.

Many unnatural elements are used to achieve a representation of an actual scene. Sand or mirrors, for example, are used to simulate water. An assortment of ceramic figures and miniature props such as bridges, buildings, etc., are used as focal points and transitions from one space to another.

Eye movements are controlled by these compositional elements; the receding diagonal lines cause the eye to zigzag as it moves from foreground elements to background. Some props and other compositional elements are intentionally placed in a forward position so that the eye is directed around them. Perhaps one sees around two rocks and then through an opening, only to discover that his vision is once again divided by two dividing valleys. In this manner, the eye is directed backwards into depth plane by plane; and then forward, or upward, again plane by plane, before it circles around the far mountain.

Such composition is not easy, nor is it quickly learned. Consequently, the addition of ceramic props and figures into the typical terrarium can be a disaster. Mr. Chang will be the first to admit that such terrarium making is more art than horticulture. In fact, some of the terrarium designs shown on these pages took as long as three days just to plan.

It is interesting to note how well the composition works within the globe shape, a shape far more complicated to work with than the typical rectangle. There is the illusion in these compositions that the scene bends around at the edges, rather like the illusion produced by mirrored globes or wide-angle photography — as though the scene were without limits. Partially this is achieved by utilizing the larger elements in the center of the composition. The use of curved lines intensifies this effect.

The utilization of diagonals, receding planes and other composition devices were utilized by Chinese painters in lieu of the mechanical perspective common to Western art. And this "flat perspective" as it were, becomes increasingly effective when it is translated into these three-dimensional scenes.

Since the main point of interest in these "Scenariums" (as Mr. Chang calls them) is the artistic arrangement, plant variety is a secondary consideration. It is best to use low light plants of a miniaturized variety so that you can keep the plants to scale. In conformity with this principle, Mr. Chang has utilized mosses as a mainstay; and so doing, has sought out picturesque mosses which are uneffected by room heat or low light. However, it has taken him years of collecting and testing wild samples to learn which will work for his purposes. Most of the mosses are from the deep forests. Mr. Chang keeps and raises them in covered refrigerator jars at light levels so low that it is difficult to believe any plant could live, much less multiply. But multiply they do, and some ten kinds of moss are now under his command.

Mr. Chang also utilizes a great deal of volcanic rock. By using the holes and convoluted forms of the rocks, he is able to provide the necessary moisture these plants require and at the same time provide interesting mountain-resembling shapes.

92

Mirrors placed below the so line create the illusion water in this pastoral scen Notice how the dam seems intensify the sense of dept while at the same tim providing a straight lir contrast to the circular el ments around it. The plan are mosses and fern

This mountain scene is mad more impressive because c the two valleys in the fore ground which afford additiona level changes. The mis effect was created by addin unnoticeable bits of spu glass. The tree-like plant are club moss

The Epidendrum tangenese, shown here almost
three times its natural size, sports a long
lasting bloom on a plant that grows to a
height of about 10 inches.

Orchids in the Terrarium

There are hundreds of orchid species suitable for the terrarium, so don't be timid about testing this largest plant family (in terms of species) in your terrarium. You will need a ventilated terrarium, full sun during the winter, and filtered sun during the other months.

Because many things about orchid culture are different, although not necessarily more difficult than other plants, you are advised to purchase one of the "growing orchids in your home" books. You can easily adapt this information to terrarium culture.

Choose your plants according to your terrarium size, sticking to the warm house species unless you have a means of keeping the temperature down. If you live in a cool climate, you can place your orchids outdoors during the summer. If you have to order through catalogs (listed in horticulture magazines), avoid the large florist type orchids which are usually listed. Ask for small species which are suitable for your particular terrarium. My experience has been that the $5 to $10 price range works just as well if not better than the more expensive plants.

These two pictures show the warmth-loving Paphiopedilum from Burma, Thailand and Vietnam. The blooms are between 2 and 3 inches in size on very short stems. These plants love moisture and make an almost ideal terrarium orchid species. When the plant is not in bloom, you have the beautifully spotted leaves to look at.

This Anoechtochilus regalis is my favorite terrarium plant. Although it is difficult to keep them more than a couple of years, they seem content in a closed terrarium with a high-light level with no hot sun.

(Left) These dwarf orchid species, shown twice their natural size, represent a new class of plants which result from the hybridization of small species. These plants are specifically intended for the home grower who has limited space. It seems that orchid growers are becoming aware of the new terrarium market.

(Below) Here the dwarf orchid species is shown natural size.

A new type of Paphios hybrid, this ground orchid grows to a height of about 10 inches, has handsome leaves and produces several blooms on each stem.

(Below) The Ludisia discolor, formerly called a Haemaria, is another ground orchid which, like Anoechtochilus regalis, is grown for its leaves. The culture is similar to the Anoechtochilus. This genus has many species with rich leaves, the most well known being the Goodyera pubescens of the Northwoods — another prized terrarium plant.

Shown larger than life, this Epidendrum porpax resides in a small brandy snifter, its home
for several years. It is necessary, however, to keep the top almost covered. The leaves you see with the orchid are fern.

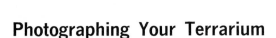

Photographing Your Terrarium

Since the terrarium provides an ever-changing scenic landscape, there is frequently a need or a desire to photograph this world of nature under glass.

Reflections

One of the most difficult problems the photographer faces is the problem of reflections. Ideally, one should use a polarizing filter over both the light source and the camera lens to minimize these trouble-some reflections. For the pictures in this book, I used a polarizing filter over the lens, but not over the light source because I felt some reflections give a truer picture of how terrariums actually appear.

In photographing the curve-shaped terrariums, I usually use direct sunlight rather than artificial light. (As long as you work quickly, the plants will not be harmed.) The sun acts as a pinpoint light source. And frequently, I will shadow the point of glare on the glass by using a small card. This method casts a small shadow on the plants, but it cuts down the reflection. If I want to illuminate a lot of sky and earth reflection, I will shoot the terrarium in the shade of a large tree and direct the sun at the container with a large mirror.

The flat-sided terrarium, such as the rectangular aquarium, produces fewer reflection problems than you have with the globe or the bottle. However, even here you will have some reflections. The simplest method to reduce them is simply to poke a hole in a piece of black cardboard and shoot through the hole. The black will not reflect in the glass. This "shooting through the hole" technique is especially useful when it is necessary to photograph a terrarium in soft sky light, for unless you put something dark behind the camera, the whole glass surface of the container will appear cloudy.

Lighting

When using artificial light, I utilize two high-power strobes. One of these strobes provides soft lighting all over, enough to show some detail in the shadows but not enough to becloud the glass; the other is focused into the terrarium by means of a piece of silver cardboard which is rolled into a tube to provide a sort of spotlight effect.

It is extremely difficult, if not downright impossible, to use a built-in flash because of the reflection problems already mentioned. And photoflood light, while not totally out of the question, would also be very difficult to work with. If you use these very hot lamps, you should move them back at least five feet away from the terrarium.

Film

I use Kodachrome II for sharpness when there is sufficient light. If the light level is not sufficient, or if I wish to retain a special mood, I use Ektachrome. Fujichrome is used when I want to bring out shades of green or blue. (You'll find that green colors take about ½ stop more exposure than regular subjects with Kodachrome, a film geared to record warm colors.)

Of course a tripod and a time exposure will reduce any problems of light quantity since you can set your exposure levels to compensate. Sometimes, I hand-hold the camera at speeds as low as 1/15 of a second. Some of the detail is lost at this speed, but I find that by doing so, I am able to create a mood of low light which seems more true to the spirit of terrariums than razor sharpness would provide.

chapter 10

Bromeliads for the Large Terrariums

Cryptanthus, such as the one shown here, are ideal in the partly open terrarium. Since these plants grow naturally upon the jungle floor, they will tolerate extreme moisture. Tolerating less light than most bromeliads, its leaves come in a wide range of colors and markings. Plants of this genus are very easy to locate in regular nurseries. The common name is Earth Stars, for the plant is somewhat star shaped.

Bromeliads for the Large Terrarium

Many bromeliad growers insist that their plants are not suitable for terrariums. The terrariums they have in mind are closed, small, very moist and placed in dark areas. And, indeed, such terrariums are not suitable for bromeliads.

However, bromeliads are not all that temperamental. They will grow in pots placed in dry houses and will flourish in moist greenhouses with ventilation. Surely somewhere between these two extremes there is a place for successful terrarium growing.

I have grown bromeliads in terrariums, in greenhouses, in the garden in frost-free areas, and in semi-desert areas where wind ripped the plastic shelter off to leave the plants exposed for three months. However, I must confess that I lost several bromeliads, but mostly because of overwatering and insufficient light.

If you plant bromeliads in your terrarium, first make sure that your terrarium is sufficiently large.

Keep the terrarium partially open; make sure the soil remains on the dry side; and provide water by spraying the leaves frequently. Make sure the plants receive full sun during the winter and filtered light during the summer. Actually, their growing conditions are almost identical to the orchid, and the two families are frequently found together.

Pictured is a Veiesea species, collected from the wilds by my plant-collecting friends in Brazil. Many of this genus enjoy home temperatures and have beautiful, marked leaves which provide good color in or out of flower.

A collection of tillandsia grows on a driftwood piece within a large ventilated terrarium. The plants are sprayed with water on sunny mornings to make sure that the plants dry by nightfall. While tillandsia are the toughest of plants — able to survive drought for long periods in exposed areas — they will not tolerate continual dampness and will quickly rot.

Cryptanthus is a fairly large plant (4 inches high; 12 inches across) which is ideally suited for terrarium life in either the closed or open container. Filtered sunlight for a few hours a day is required to bring out the best of its rose coloring. It is a color-selected variety of a ground-growing bromeliad. This plant can be propagated in both soil and in sphagnum, although the moss seems to provide far better results.

Spanish moss, the beauty or scourge of the South (depending upon how you look at it), is another bromeliad which requires air circulation, a medium-high-light level and sufficient moisture. Since this is a fast grower under the proper conditions, it may need periodic thinning. If it seems a bit dry in your particular terrarium, spray the plant on sunny mornings.

This tillandsia species, like most, has a gray-white coating of cells which absorb and retain water from fog and dew. This plant is common to jungle tree tops and has been found growing on telephone wires. As you might imagine, the roots do more to hold the plant in place than supply it with its nutrients.

This is another tillandsia species of a more compressed habit. The small blooms last only a short time but the rose-colored bracts often retain their color for months.

Where to Buy Terrarium Plants

During my twenty years of terrarium experience, the availability of grand terrarium plants has never been better than it is today. The upsurge in plant interest has spawned a new kind of store — the plant boutique — where you will find the more common terrarium plants in abundance. To locate and purchase the rare and unusual plants, however, you will have to be more inventive. One obvious source for these more difficult-to-find terrarium plants is the mail-order house, many of which are listed in the back of this book. Ordering plants by mail is occasionally the only means by which a person can get his hands on many of the best plants. The method is time consuming, but it can be fun. Send for the catalog and when it arrives, you can spend hours pouring over the endless names and descriptions. Don't be frightened by the Latin names; they are harmless. Neither should you worry about ordering plants which you may never have seen nor heard of before.

If you intend to plant as soon as your order arrives at your door, the best time to order from a catalog is during the spring. Spring ordering insures that the plants will have time to recover from the severe shock of transportation in time for the active summer growth period. Fall ordering is advised for those who want to plant the new arrivals in pots for a few months to let them get started. Although the main growth period is during the spring and summer months, you will probably notice new growth much earlier. During the short days of autumn and winter, the plants tend to remain passive and dormant; but as the days begin to grow longer, you may notice new shoots as early as the second week in January. Plants are not generally shipped during the cold months of winter, expecially in the northern colder climates. And summer can be a bad time to ship plants since there is always the possibility of exposure to undue heat.

Before your plants arrive, you should get your terrarium ready. Have all the elements at hand and the planting mix moistened so that you are ready to make an immediate home for the new arrivals.

If, for some reason, you do not intend to transfer the new plants to your terrarium immediately, you should make sure that all of the leaves are covered with damp newspaper and that the leaves are well exposed to light and air. It is best, of course, to place the packages (just as they are) inside the terrarium for protection, making sure that they receive no full sun. Stored in this manner, they will usually hold out for a few days without harm until you have time to do the actual planting work.

If the newly arrived plants have broken stems and leaves, you should keep them slightly drier than you ordinarily would as a safeguard against root rot. Watch the new plants closely for rot, removing any

stems or leaves that show signs of it. In fact, if you have damaged plants, it is generally best to store them in a quarantine terrarium for several days before final planting. This method will give you a better opportunity to deal with problems which might develop at this sensitive point in culture.

In most cases, the plants that arrive will be green, full and healthy. However, if you have never ordered plants by mail before, you should be aware that sometimes the plants which arrive do not match up to the majestic visions you had in mind. They are sometimes far smaller than you had imagined; sometimes the leaves have been bent out of shape or have yellowed; or, perhaps, some of the leaves have actually fallen off. Commercial packing requires that the plants be dug in lots, orders being filled from bins; and the plants may be left for days before actual packing and shipping. When ordering, you should keep in mind that these plants will possibly not be perfect plants that will look as though they have just been taken out of the greenhouse; they are, rather, merely stock plants which, like anything else that has had to undergo a long and difficult journey, may show signs of wear and tear. There is no need to be apprehensive since all reputable firms will replace severely damaged plants without charge. However, when you want to sample or test the quality of a mail-order house, it is best to send only a small order.

I have found that the places which have the most attractive and inspiring catalogs do not necessarily send the best plants. Also, there seems to be no absolute correlation between how far the plants have to travel and what kind of condition they will be in when they arrive. My experience has been that nursery stock from 100 miles away is not necessarily fresher than stock which comes from the opposite coast.

For those who wish to ship plants to friends or relatives, I will share a method which has worked well for me. My trick is to place the plant into an inflated plastic bag which is tied at the top. Then, I fashion some cardboard braces and place them snugly around the plastic in a box. Now the box can be tossed about without moving the soil or my plant. If you do have to ship plants, remember that plants should be shipped immediately after packing.

As a rule of thumb, whenever possible, it is better to select plants from a growing situation where you can see what you are getting and avoid the shock (for both you and your plant) that often accompanies shipping. Then, those plants which you can't find locally can be ordered.

One good local source is the rare-plant nursery. As businesses go, they are rather rare specimens themselves. In fact, the rare-plant nurseries with which

I am well acquainted are run for love rather than profit; owners tend to be dedicated, finely honed to their subject and a bit eccentric.

In most instances, these nurseries are not terrarium specialists, but they do include terrarium material among their enormous variety of plants; and from the literally thousands of individual species in stock, you will certainly be able to find something you want. Some people contend that plants from such places are outrageously expensive. I have never found this to be true. In my opinion, considering the enormous inventory and the work involved, the prices are very reasonable. What you are paying for, of course, is not just the single plant, but the stock maintenance of their enormous inventory. Besides, a small $5 plant will grow and make divisions fairly quickly.

Certainly one of the greatest advantages of visiting the rare plant nurseries, or those that specialize in terrarium plants, is that you can see firsthand exactly how these plants are professionally grown.

ACKNOWLEDGEMENTS

Glass Containers: GEARY'S
351 N. Beverly Dr.
Beverly Hills, CA 90210
THE ATTIC
8159 West Third
Los Angeles, CA 90048

Plastic Boxes: ART SERVICES
8221 Melrose Ave.
Los Angeles, CA 90046

Orchids: ARMACOST & ROYSTON, INC.
11920 La Grange Ave.
West Los Angeles, CA 90025
FRED A. STEWART'S, INC.
1212 E. Las Tunas Dr.
San Gabriel, CA 91776

Plants: FUCHSIA LAND
4629 Centinela Ave.
Los Angeles, CA 90066
OAKHURST GARDENS
345 W. Colorado
Arcadia, CA 91006

Societies:
THE AMERICAN ORCHID SOCIETY, INC.
Botanical Museum of Harvard University
Cambridge, Mass. 02138

THE AMERICAN BEGONIA SOCIETY
Dept. H
1949 S. Manchester Blvd.
Anaheim, CA 92805

THE AMERICAN BONSAI SOCIETY
Corresponding Membership
229 Northshore Dr.
Lake Waukomis
Parkville, Missouri 64151

THE AMERICAN ROCK GARDEN SOCIETY
Richard W. Redfield
Box 26
Closter, New Jersey 07624

THE AMERICAN HORTICULTURAL SOCIETY
Mt. Vernon, Virginia 22121

Plant Sources of Supply

CALIFORNIA

Abbey Garden 18007 Topham St. Reseda, CA 91335	Cacti and succulents; Catalog
Antonelli Bros. 2545 Capitola Rd. Santa Cruz, CA 95010	Gesneriads and begonias
Beach Garden Nursery 2131 Portola Dr. Santa Cruz, CA 95060	Bromeliads and exotics; No shipping
Beahm Gardens 2686 Pamoa St. Pasadena, CA 91107	Cacti and succulents; Catalog free
Bolduc's Greenhill Nursery 2131 Vallejo St. St. Helena, CA 94574	Exotic ferns
Cactus by Mueller 10411 Rosedale Highway Bakersfield, CA 93307	List 10¢
California Jungle Gardens 11977 San Vicente Blvd. West Los Angeles, CA 90049	Bromeliads and other tropicals
Dos Pueblos Orchid Co. Box 158 Goleta, CA 93017	Orchids; Catalog
The Green House 9515 Flower St. Bellflower, CA 90706	African violets, gesneriads; supplies
Henrietta's Nursery 1345 N. Brawley Ave. Fresno, CA 93705	Cacti and succulents; Catalog 50¢
Johnson Cactus Gardens Paramount, CA 90723	Cacti and succulents; Catalog 10¢
Jungle Plants & Flowers Box 389 Culver City, CA 90230	Bromeliads
Kent's Bromeliads 6518 Bedford Ave. Los Angeles, CA 90056	List 35¢
Leatherman's Gardens 2637 N. Lee Ave. South El Monte, CA 91733	Ferns
Rod McLellan Co. 1450 El Camino Real South San Francisco, CA 94080	Orchids Catalog
Marz Bromeliads 10782 Citrus Dr. Moorpark, CA 93021	List 20¢
Oakhurst Gardens 345 Colorado Blvd. Arcadia, CA 91006	Carnivorous plants and exotic bulbs
Clyde Robin Box 2091 Castro Valley, CA 94546	Wildflowers Catalog 50¢
Seaborn Del Dios Nursery Route 3, Box 455 Escondido, CA 92025	Bromeliads Catalog $1.00
Taylor's Herb Garden 2649 Stingl Rosemead, CA 91770	

Van Ness Water Gardens
2460 N. Euclid Ave.
Upland, CA 91786 — Aquatic plants

West Coast Gesneriads
2179 44th Ave.
San Francisco, CA 94116 — Gesneriads No shipping

CANADA

Harborcrest Nurseries
1425 Benvenuto Ave.
Victoria, B.C., Canada — Gesneriads

COLORADO

Craven's Greenhouse
4732 W. Tennessee
Denver, CO — African violets and other gesneriads

CONNECTICUT

Buell's Greenhouses
Eastford, CT 06242 — Gloxinias and other gesneriads Catalog $1.00

Caprilands Herb Farm
Coventry, CT 06238 — Herb seeds and plants Lists

Grass Roots, Ltd.
8 Crestview
Bloomfield, CT 06002 — Plants; supplies

J & L Orchids
20 Sherwood Rd.
Easton, CT 06812 — Botanical orchids

Lauray of Salisbury
Under Mountain Rd.
Salisbury, CT 06068 — Gesneriads, begonias, succulents and other houseplants; list

Logee's Greenhouses
Danielson, CT 06239 — Begonias, gesneriads, varied foliage and blooming houseplants; Catalog 50¢

Oliver Nurseries
1159 Bronson Rd.
Fairfield, CT 06430 — Evergreens for rock gardens

FLORIDA

Alberts & Merkel Bros., Inc.
Box 537
Boynton Beach, FL 33435 — Orchids, bromeliads, and other tropical plants; Catalog 50¢

Bennett's Bromeliads & Bonsai
1621 Mayfield Ave.
Winter Park, FL 32789 — Send stamped, addressed envelope for list

Mrs. E. Reed Brelsford
1816 Cherry St.
Jacksonville, FL 32205 — Exotic ferns

John Brudy
Box 64
Cocoa Beach, FL 32931 — Rare shrub seeds and plants, succulents; list

Burt's Nursery
Box 776
Jupiter, FL 33458 — Bromeliads, tropical plants

Cornelison Bromeliad Nursery
225 San Bernardino St.
N. Fort Meyers, FL 33903

Fantastic Gardens
9550 S.W. 67th Ave.
South Miami, FL 33156 — Bromeliads, ferns, exotic foliage; No shipping

Fennell Orchid Co., Inc.
26715 S.W. 157 Ave.
Homestead, FL 33030 — Orchids

Goochland Nurseries, Inc.
Pembroke, FL 33866 — Indoor plant list

Jones & Scully
2200 N.W. 33rd Ave.
Miami, FL 33142 — Orchids; Catalog $1.00

H. Presner
Box 10
Coral Gables, FL 33134 — Bonsai dwarf trees

Slocum Water Gardens
1101 Cypress Garden Rd.
Winter Haven, FL 33880 — Aquatic plants

ILLINOIS

Hauserman's Orchids
Box 363
Elmhurst, IL 60218 — Orchids — wide selection

INDIANA

Susan Feece
Box 9479
Walkerton, IN 46574 — African violets and gesneriads

Novel Plants
Bridgeton, IN 47836 — Houseplants; Catalog 10¢

Quality Violet House
Box 947
Walkerton, IN 46574 — Gesneriads

Tropical Gardens
Route 1, Box 143
Greenwood, IN 46142 — Houseplants

Wilson Bros.
Roachdale, IN 46172 — Geraniums; Catalog

KANSAS

Cook's Geranium Nursery
712 N. Grand
Lyons, KS 67554 — Geraniums; Catalog 25¢

Ben Haines
1902 Lane
Topeka, KS 60664 — Cacti and succulents; List $1.00

Payne's Violets & Gesneriads
6612 Leavenworth Rd.
Kansas City, KS 66104

Tropical Paradise Greenhouse
8825 W. 79th St.
Overland Park, KS 66104 — Miniature plants — wide selection

KENTUCKY

Milburn O. Button
Route 1, Box 386
Crestwood, KY 40014 — Gesneriad seed

MAINE

Goodwill Garden
Route 1
Scarborough, ME 04074 — Alpines

Merry Gardens
Camden, ME 04843 — Houseplants; Catalog $1.00

MARYLAND

Kensington Orchids, Inc.
33101 Plyers Mill Rd.
Kensington, MD 20795 — Orchids

Three Springs Fisheries
Lilypons, MD 21717 — Aquatic plants

MASSACHUSETTS

Arthur E. Allgrove
279 Woburn St.
N. Wilmington, MA 01888 — Native plants, carnivorous species; Supplies; Catalog 25¢

P. De Jager & Sons, Inc.
188 Ashbury St.
S. Hamilton, MA 01982 — Bulb selection

Alexander Irving Heimlich
71 Burlington St.
Woburn, MA 01801 — Bulbs

Kartuz Greenhouses
92 Chestnut St.
Wilmington, MA 01887 — Miniature plants; Catalog 25¢

Leslie's Wildflower Nursery
30 Summer St.
Methuen, MA 01884 — Wildflowers

Paradise Gardens
14 May St.
Whitman, MA 02382 — Aquatic plants

MICHIGAN

Burgess Seed & Plant Co., Inc.
67 E. Battle Creek St.
Galesburg, MI 49053 — Miniature plants; carnivorous species; Catalog

Margaret Ilgenfritz Orchids
Box 665
Monroe, MI 48161 — Miniature orchids; Catalog 25¢

Mary's African Violets
19788 San Juan
Detroit, MI 48221 — African violets; Supplies

MISSOURI

J's African Violets
6932 Wise Ave.
St. Louis, MO 63139

African violets;
Supplies

Mrs. Bert Routh
Lewisburg, MO 65685

Gesneriads

Mrs. Leonard Volkart
Russelville, MO 65074

African violets and
episcias

NEBRASKA

Engert's Violet House
7457 Schuyler Dr.
Omaha, NB 68114

African violets and
other gesneriads

NEW JERSEY

Barrington Greenhouses
860 Clemente Rd.
Barrington, NJ 08016

Miniature houseplants

Charbet Nursery
7 Toucan Court
Wayne, NJ 07470

Houseplants and
gesneriads

Fischer Greenhouses
Linwood, NJ 08221

African violets and
other gesneriads;
Catalog 25¢

Jones Nursery
Hazlet, NJ 07730

Gesneriads

Lager & Hurrell
426 Morris Ave.
Summit, NJ 07901

Orchids;
Catalog $2.00

Plant Oddities
Box 127
Basking Ridge, NJ 07920

Carnivorous plants;
Catalog 25¢

Roehrs Exotic Nurseries
Route 2, Box 144
Farmingdale, NJ 07727

Houseplants;
No shipping

Scotsward Violet Farm
71 Hanover Rd.
Florham Park, NJ 07932

African violets

NEW MEXICO

New Mexico Cactus Research
Box 787
Belen, NM 87002

Cactus seed

NEW YORK

Aunt Dotty's Arbor
1103 Third Ave.
New York, NY 10021

Orchids;
No shipping

Farm & Garden Nursery
116 Reade St.
New York, NY 10013

Foliage and bloom
plants;
Supplies

Lyndon Lyon
14 Mutchler St.
Dolgeville, NY 13329

African violets and
gesneriads;
List

Mayfair Nurseries
Route 2
Nichols, NY 13812

Dwarf conifers and
shrubs

Peter Paul's Nursery
Macedon Rd.
Canandaigua, NY 14424

Catalog 25¢

Whistling Hill Greenhouses
Box 27
Hamburg, NY 16075

Gesneriads;
List

Wyrtzen Exotic Plants
165 Bryant Ave.
Floral Park, NY 11001

Begonias and gesneriads;
List

NORTH CAROLINA

The Garden Nook
Highway No. 1
Raleigh, NC

Exotic plants

Williford's Nursery
Route 3
Smithfield, NC 27577

Houseplants;
Catalog 20¢

OHIO

L. Easterbrook Greenhouses
Butler, OH 44822

African violets and
other gesneriads;
List 50¢

Granger Gardens
Route 2
Wilbur Rd.
Medina, OH 44256

Gesneriads;
List 50¢

McComb's Greenhouses
New Straitsville, OH 43766

Houseplants

OREGON

Arndt's Floral Garden
20454 N.E. Sandy Blvd.
Troutdale, OR 97060

Exotic plants;
List 10¢

Spidell's Fine Plants
Box 93D
Junction City, OR 97448

African violets and
gesneriads;
List

Siskiyou Rare Plant Nursery
522 Franquette St.
Medford, OR 97501

Alpines and rock
plants;
Catalog 50¢

PENNSYLVANIA

W. Atlee Burpee Co.
Philadelphia, PA 19132

Seeds; Supplies

Chester Hills Orchids
Route 2
Catfish Lane
Pottstown, PA 19464

Orchids

Conrad-Pyle
West Grove, PA 19390

Miniature roses

Greenland Flower Shop
Port Matilda, PA 16870

Houseplants;
Catalog 25¢

Tinari Greenhouses
2325 Valley Rd.
Huntingdon Valley, PA 19006

African violets and
other gesneriads;

RHODE ISLAND

Greene Herb Gardens
Greene, RI 02827

List

SOUTH CAROLINA

George W. Park Seed Co.
64 Cokesbury Rd.
Greenwood, SC 29646

Houseplants and seeds;
Catalog

TENNESSEE

Gesneriad Jungle
2507 Washington Pike
Knoxville, TN 37917

List

Savage Gardens
Box 163
McMinnville, TN 37110

Woodland terrarium
plants;
List — return envelope

TEXAS

Desert Plant Company
Box 880
Marfa, TX 79843

Cactus list

Volkmann Bros. Greenhouses
2714 Minert Street
Dallas, TX 75219

African violets and
houseplants;
Supplies

VERMONT

Sky-Cleft Gardens
Camp St. Ext.
Barre, VT 05641

Rock plants

WASHINGTON

Dee's Garden
E-3803 19th Ave.
Spokane, WA 99203

Gesneriads

Norvell Greenhouses
318 S. Greenacres Rd.
Greenacres, WA 99016

Foliage and bloom
plants;
Catalog 25¢

Mt. Rainier Alpine Gardens
2007 S. 126 St.
Seattle, WA 98168

Dwarf conifers;
rhododendrons and
alpines

WISCONSIN

Harvey J. Ridge
1126 Arthur St.
Wausau, WI 54401

African violets and
other exotic plants;
Supplies

Printed in U.S.A.

ISBN 0-87294-053-5